Sedra Scenes

SKITS FOR EVERY TORAH PORTION

Stan J. Beiner

A.R.E. Publishing, Inc.
Springfield, New Jersey

DEDICATION

This anniversary edition is dedicated to my wife, Judith and my three daughters Zoe, Adina, and Erin. You make life worth living.

Cover Artwork

"MATAN TORAH"
by Tamar Messer

"*Matan Torah*" ("The gift of Torah") depicts the moment of revelation at Mount Sinai. According to the traditional midrash, at that moment everything was silent — the people, the animals, the birds — even the air stood still. The bright red sky emphasizes the hot, dry desert air. Moses holds the tablets high as the Israelites raise their hands in gratitude to receive this wondrous gift.

Tamar Messer, born in Haifa, is a well-known and loved Israeli artist. The distinctly vivid and colorful style of her work draws upon a spirit of vitality that speaks directly to the hearts of the young and young at heart. Tamar's work has been exhibited in numerous group and single exhibitions, among them a long-term exhibition in the Israel Museum in Jerusalem. Her work represented the State of Israel in an international exhibition in London in 2000, and won first prize. Besides illustrating for the Israeli newspapers *Yedioth Achronot* and *Ma'ariv*, she has done illustrations for numerous books. In addition to her work as an artist, Tamar leads a new generation of young artists as a lecturer at the WITZO — Canada Nerri Blumfield School of Art and Design, one of the most prestigious art and design schools in Israel.

Contact Tamar Messer through her website at www.tamarsgallery.co.il.

© Copyright A.R.E. Publishing, Inc. 2002

Published by:
A.R.E. Publishing, Inc.
An imprint of Behrman House — Millburn, New Jersey
www.behrmanhouse.com

Library of Congress Catalog Card Number 82-71282
ISBN 10: 0-86705-077-1
ISBN13: 978-0-86705-077-6

Printed in the United States of America
10 9 8 7 6 5 4 3

Table of Contents

INTRODUCTION

It was 1980 and I was the assistant program director at Gindling Hilltop Camp in Malibu, California. Imagine spending Shabbat on the top of a hill facing out over the Pacific Ocean with a crystal blue sky as the backdrop and the scent of the sea in the air. The only thing between me and a totally spiritual connection with my Maker was the sight of one hundred campers with blank faces staring past me as Torah was read from the rustic pulpit. The disconnection to the service was frustrating, and as the Jewish educator, I was faced with the challenge of finding a solution.

A "light bulb"moment! Having always enjoyed writing skits, I put my hand to work at developing a play on that week's *sedra*. Throughout the week, I cajoled and begged campers to be in the skit. It would be fun, I pleaded. It'll make you popular, I teased. When the play was performed the following Shabbat morning, the response surprised me. Not only did the campers connect with the service, but they wanted to be a part of it the following week! More plays followed, and the formula began to take shape.

The next year, as a teacher at the Stephen S. Wise Day School in Los Angeles, I continued to produce skits while teaching Torah. Drama became a valuable medium for engaging students and campers intellectually, emotionally, and physically. While the number of books containing plays has grown over the years, at that time, little existed in this genre to assist educators in promoting enthusiasm for and interest in Torah.

Encouraged by many to publish my work, I confidently sent out manuscripts to various Jewish publishers. Several months later, I had no room on my bedroom door for all the rejection notices I had taped up. Essentially, the publishers shared with me the fact that plays don't sell. It was a humbling experience. As fate would have it, I happened to attend services at Temple Sinai in Denver while visiting old friends in 1980. Rabbi Ray Zwerin, then President of A.R.E., took me aside and told me that he had liked the humor and saw possibilities in the format. Two years later, *Sedra Scenes* went to print for the first time. It was an instant hit, and a best-seller by Jewish education standards.

The guidance received from Rabbi Zwerin and Audrey Friedman Marcus led to the creation of a book that has now entertained and taught thousands of Jewish adults and kids. I thank these two very special people for helping raise this medium to a level not realized prior to the publication of *Sedra Scenes.*

A goal of Bible education is to present the characters of the Torah as real human beings. As educators, we want our students to be aware that the problems and concerns that our biblical ancestors faced still exist today. In order to foster this awareness, it is first necessary to catch our students' attention and imagination. One such strategy is the use of drama.

HOW TO USE THIS BOOK

For those being introduced to *Sedra Scenes* for the first time, the book is composed of a series of brief skits, one on each weekly Torah portion, written with contemporary language and perspective so that they will appeal to old and young alike. While the scripts use humor to motivate, each is based on, and emphasizes, the themes of the biblical text. Junior and senior high school students, as well as sophisticated fifth and sixth graders, will relate to the language and perspective of these contemporary playlets.

Appropriate Settings
The skits in this book can be used successfully in a variety of settings. These include:

Day Schools: The skits can be used as a supplement when studying the text, to emphasize major points and to provide a change of pace.

Supplementary Schools: *Sedra Scenes* serves as an enjoyable, easy to understand vehicle for introducing students who have little or no background to the characters and events of the Torah. Each week, the skit for the appropriate Torah portion can be read by students and followed by a brief discussion. If a particular *parashah* is being studied for several sessions, it may be effective to use the script as an introduction in the first lesson and again as a summation when concluding the unit. The material in *Sedra Scenes* thus enables teachers to plan an effective 10-20 minute segment devoted to the weekly *parashah*. If more time is available, students can also read and analyze the text itself using a variety of commentaries.

Weekend Retreats, Shabbatonim, Camps, Junior Congregation, Youth Group: The skits can be used in any of these settings to enhance Shabbat services, to help explain the Torah portion, to enrich the Judaic component of the program, and/or for sheer entertainment.

Whatever the setting, introducing *Sedra Scenes* on a regular basis will help students learn and internalize events and personalities in the order they occur in the Torah, as well as appreciate the sweep and importance of the biblical characters, events, laws, and concepts.

Presenting the Skits

In just five or ten minutes, with few if any props, with little or no preparation, a group of students can perform *Parashat HaShavua*. A variety of options is possible for presenting these skits:

Theatre Performance: *Sedra Scenes* can be staged with props and costumes.

Reader's Theater: The characters, lined up shoulder to shoulder, can read their parts without any movement.

Classroom: Students can be assigned to read parts from their seats.

Puppet Show: For an enjoyable change of format, groups can present the skits in a puppet setting.

Plays can be performed by a group of students for other classes, for shut-ins, for groups of parents, or simply for each other. The staging can be as simple or as complicated as desired, depending on the discretion of the leader, the available time and resources, and the purpose of the production. Staging directions are not included in the text. It is generally best to keep the production simple and to work out the details among the performers.

When using *Sedra Scenes* as a teaching tool, each player should have a copy of the book of skits in order to assure a smooth reading.

In the Torah itself, scenes often change abruptly. Such a change of scene is noted in this book by the use of the symbol * * *. In performing the skits, scene changes can be indicated by merely shifting attention from one center of action to another.

CONCLUSION

This book, unlike its subject, is not cast in stone or set on parchment. Many players may read a few parts, or few actors can perform many parts. Words and paragraphs may be deleted and whole sections added as needed. Students can write their own skits based on their experiences with the ones in this book. The intent of this collection is to serve as a new educational vehicle and to provide a fresh look at what is the central focus of our heritage.

Beresheet בראשית

CAST
GOD
NARRATOR
ADAM
EVE
SNAKE
ABEL
CAIN

GOD: Hello down there? That's silly. Who am I talking to? There isn't anyone down there. There isn't even a "down there" down there! Boy, it sure is dark — I think I'll turn on some lights.

NARRATOR: And God said: "Let there be light," and there was light. And God saw that it was good. God called the light "day," and the darkness God called "night." And there was evening and there was morning, a first day.

GOD: That's better. Would you look at this universe? I think I'll do some redecorating. Everything looks so disorganized!

NARRATOR: God said: "Let there be space between the waters." God made an expanse and separated it from the water. God called the expanse "sky." And there was evening and morning, the second day.

GOD: This is fun! I should have done this long ago. A little bit more remodeling — I like that. And let me put some plants here to give this place a fancy touch.

NARRATOR: God said: "Let the water be gathered in one area so that dry land appears." God saw it was good and said, "Let

1

the earth bring forth vegetation, plants and trees of every kind."

GOD: Did I do all that already?

NARRATOR: It says so right here in the Book.

GOD: The Torah?

NARRATOR: Right.

GOD: If it says so in the Torah, it must be so. I'm glad I had all this written down!

NARRATOR: And there was evening and morning, the third day.

GOD: Let Me take a look at the list. I have trees, earth, sky, water, and light. I think the lighting has to be better at night. A few of these should do it.

NARRATOR: And God said: "Let there be lights in the sky to serve as set times for days and years." And God created the sun, the moon and the stars. God saw it was good. And there was evening and morning, the fourth day.

GOD: Now, I'm making progress! This place looks great, but I need some moving things . . . some action. Birds, we need lots of birds! And sea creatures, too. And I'll top it off with some living creatures on land. Look at them all together. They are so cute!

NARRATOR: God said: "Let the waters bring forth swarms of living creatures and birds that fly and great sea monsters." And it was good. And there was evening and morning, the fifth day.

GOD: Wouldn't it be nice to have someone to talk to? I'll make someone in My image. Here's some clay. He looks kind

of funny with three arms. Maybe I can put one in the back . . .
nope. Good for scratching, but strange. I'll go with two arms.

NARRATOR: God said: "Let us make man in our image." And
God said to him, "Be fruitful and multiply, and you shall rule
the birds, the fish, and all living things on earth." And God saw
it was good. And there was evening and morning, the sixth day.
And God stopped working and rested on the seventh day and
called it Shabbat. And Shabbat was holy.

* * *

GOD: Adam, how are things going?

ADAM: I'm bored. I've named all the animals. They're all quite
nice, but frankly, I feel like a babysitter. There's nobody to talk
to.

GOD: Go to sleep, Adam. This will take no time at all. Scalpel.
Wrench, Knife, Hammer. This rib should do it. A little clay and
dust, some sugar and spice . . . perfect! Adam, wake up.

ADAM: What happened?

GOD: Adam, meet Eve. Eve, meet Adam.

ADAM: Wow! Hello, beautiful. How about a stroll in the
Garden of Eden?

EVE: I'd love to.

GOD: By the way, stay away from the Tree of Immortal Life
and the Tree of the Knowledge of Good and Evil. You can eat
from any other trees. Don't stay up too late.

BOTH: We won't.

* * *

SNAKE: Pssst. Over here.

EVE: Hi. Can I help you?

SNAKE: I'm selling raffles for the Boy Scouts. Want to buy one?

ADAM: Boy Scouts?

EVE: Raffles?

ADAM: What are you talking about?

SNAKE: Are you people dumb? Wait a second — I'll bet you haven't eaten from the Tree of Knowledge.

EVE: We're not supposed to do that.

SNAKE: Don't be ridiculous! A cute girl like you should know the score. It's such good tasting fruit! One bite can't hurt. Have a fruit and buy a raffle.

EVE: Well, one bite won't hurt.

SNAKE: It's pretty good.

EVE: It sure is! Adam, take a bite.

ADAM: It's delicious!

BOTH: Ooops!

EVE: Adam, you don't have any clothes on!

ADAM: Neither do you.

SNAKE: Gosh, you two are very clever.

ADAM: Quick, cover yourself!

4

GOD: Adam? Adam? I was worried about you. What's this? You dropped the core. One should never litter. Why are you hiding like that?

EVE: We're naked!

GOD: I know that, but you're not supposed to know that. Let me see that piece of fruit. Uh-oh. Snake! Where are you?

SNAKE: Gotta go! I have a dentist appointment.

GOD: Snake, stay where you are!

ADAM: Are we in trouble?

EVE: We're in trouble.

GOD: Snake, for what you did, you shall be cursed. You shall crawl on your belly. As for you, Eve, giving birth will be painful.

ADAM: Please! Give us another chance!

GOD: There are no second chances in the Garden of Eden. You shall now have to work for a living. You are hereby kicked out of the Garden of Eden.

* * *

NARRATOR: And Adam and Eve had a son, and they named him Cain. And Eve bore a second son, and they called him Abel. And Cain became a farmer and Abel was a shepherd.

ABEL: It happened like this. I brought my best lamb to be sacrificed to God. I wanted to thank God for a good year. Cain says, "Hey, Abel, I'm coming too." So he picks up some grains from the ground and joins me. I say, "Cain, God won't like your offering," but Cain was lazy. We get to the altar and offer our sacrifices. I offer my lamb and Cain his simple grains.

5

Guess what? God doesn't accept Cain's sacrifice, but loves mine. So what does Cain do? He picks up a rock and kills me. He always did have a temper. So I became the first murder victim. Cain could be so hotheaded.

GOD: Cain? Where is your brother?

CAIN: How should I know? Am I my brother's keeper?

GOD: You killed your brother.

CAIN: It was an accident.

GOD: You call dropping a rock on someone's head an accident?

CAIN: I was aiming for the fly on Abel's shoulder.

GOD: You're talking to the Creator — I make up the stories, not you. For your sin, you are destined always to wander. You can never settle down. You must wander the face of the earth.

NARRATOR: And so it was that Cain wandered. And Adam and Eve had another son, and they named him Seth. And the people of the earth began to multiply. But they began to do evil things, and God said that it was time to wipe them off the face of the earth. Only Noah found favor in God's eyes.

Noah

נֹחַ

CAST
NARRATOR
GOD
NOAH
SHEM
HAM
JAPHETH
ANNOUNCER
RAVEN
DOVE
PERSON 1
PERSON 2
PERSON 3
PERSON 4

NARRATOR: The earth became corrupt before God; the earth was filled with lawlessness.

GOD: Would you look at this mess? Adam and Eve eat of the Tree of Knowledge and everything goes down the drain. I've got to do something about this. Maybe I'll blow up the whole place. No, I can't do that — I guess, deep down, I'm a softy. There are still a few good people. Not many, but a few. Yet, something must be done.

NOAH: Any luck, Shem?

SHEM: Nope.

NOAH: How about you, Japheth?

JAPHETH: Not a single customer.

7

NOAH: Ham, any luck?

HAM: Sorry, Dad.

NOAH: I can't understand it. I thought for sure we'd make a fortune in the cruise line business.

JAPHETH: The problem is that we live in the desert. No one takes cruises across the desert.

NOAH: Well, I've been working on that problem. If it ever rains, we'll just build a dam, put the boat behind it, and float around our own lake.

HAM: Dad, you're dreaming! We just picked the wrong business to be in. We should go back to being nomads.

GOD: Noah?

NOAH: Quiet sons, I think we've got a customer.

GOD: Noah?

JAPHETH: Excuse me, Sir, but I can't seem to see you. Where are you?

GOD: Here, there, everywhere. Listen, Noah, I want to charter a cruise.

NOAH: Terrific! When would you like to go?

GOD: Soon.

NOAH: Soon? We're sort of waiting for the rainy season. We're a little short on water.

GOD: You need some rain? I can arrange that.

NOAH: You can arrange for rain? You must be God.

GOD: At your service.

NOAH: Oh dear! Oh my goodness!

GOD: Relax, Noah. I've got a job for you. I want you to build an ark.

NOAH: We have a boat already.

GOD: Boats are easy. I want an ark. Make it out of gopher wood, cover it inside and out with pitch. Make it three stories high, and put strong floors on the second and third decks.

NOAH: Who is taking this cruise? The Missus? The kids?

GOD: Listen, Noah. You're a nice guy. A little strange, but you're the best I've got. I'm about to give the earth a bath. This place is about to go under. I'm opening the floodgates in the sky. I'm offering you and your family a free ride. You're the only ones I'm saving.

NOAH: What can I say?

GOD: You've said enough. Get working. I'm anxious to get this flood on the road. By the way, send some of your boys to gather up one pair of each kind of animal, and seven pairs of all clean animals, and put them on board also.

NOAH: Out of the question. I will not permit animals on one of my cruises.

GOD: Noah!

NOAH: On the other hand, I was just saying how nice it would be to take a cruise with a camel.

NARRATOR: And Noah did just as the Almighty had commanded him. Noah was six hundred years old when the flood came. All the fountains of the great deep burst apart, and the floodgates of the sky broke open.

ANNOUNCER: Ladies and gentlemen, welcome to day 40 of the crisis in Mesopotamia. It's been raining for forty days and forty nights. The waters have covered the highest mountain. Noah and his family are hostages at sea.

SHEM: Dad, these animals are beginning to smell a bit!

NOAH: Ham was supposed to buy some air freshener at the market before we left.

HAM: Sorry, Dad. I forgot.

NOAH: Well, look who's laughing last! Everyone made fun of Noah's Cruise in the Sand. Just wait 'till I see them!

JAPHETH: Dad, they won't be there. We're the only ones left in the world.

NOAH: I keep forgetting.

NARRATOR: And when the waters had swelled on the earth for one hundred and fifty days, God remembered Noah and all the animals with him. And God caused the wind to blow across the earth, and the waters subsided. And the ark came to rest on the mountains of Ararat.

NOAH: Open the window. Good. Now gimme the bird. No, not the ostrich! The raven. Okay, little birdy. Go see if there's dry land out there.

RAVEN: Great! I can hardly wait to get out of here. Wow! Water, water, everywhere, but I'm not going back to that ark.

NARRATOR: Then Noah sent the dove, but the dove returned. He waited another seven days, and sent the dove forth again.

DOVE: What a bully. The elephants weren't doing anything. Does he send them? Nooooo. But me, he sends twice! Hey, what have we here? A branch. Boy, will Noah be surprised!

NARRATOR: And the dove returned with an olive branch. Noah waited seven more days, and sent the dove forth again.

DOVE: This is ridiculous. Three times! I'm not coming back. I'm heading for Palm Springs. So long, fellas!

NARRATOR: And the dove returned no more, and Noah removed the covering of the ark and he saw that the ground was drying.

GOD: Come out, Noah. The weather is beautiful!

NOAH: It's over!

GOD: That's right. But I will hate to see this month's water bill.

NOAH: I've been thinking. Here I am, little ole Noah, starting the whole world over again. Suppose we get off track in the future — are you going to zap us again?

GOD: No, I promise not to flood the entire earth again. I'll create a covenant between you and Me. This shall be a sign of our agreement forever.

NOAH: A second moon? How nice.

GOD: Dull. It needs some color. Let's try a rainbow. There — one rainbow. It's beautiful! Sometimes I amaze even Myself.

* * *

NARRATOR: And the rainbow became an everlasting covenant between people and God. And Noah's sons spread throughout the world, and seventy nations grew out of them.

And everyone started begetting everyone. And everyone spoke the same language.

ANNOUNCER: Attention! Listen, everybody. Let's build a tower to reach God.

PERSON 1: Together we shall reach the sky!

GOD: Would you look at that? Those nuts are at it again. They'll never learn. I have a good mind to zap them, but I can't do that anymore. Let me think . . . I've got it! This will mix them up.

PERSON 2: Pass the bricks.

PERSON 3: Je ne comprend pas.

PERSON 4: Talk Sumerian!

PERSON 3: Sprechen sie deutsch?

PERSON 4: Hey, Nahar, would you find out what's going on?

PERSON 2: Ani lo mayveen!

NARRATOR: And God confounded their speech so they could not understand each other, and they spread out over the earth. That is why they stopped building the tower. They called it Babel because God confounded speech and spread people over the world.

GOD: Now that was much more clever than the flood!

* * *

NARRATOR: And Terach lived in the land of Ur and he had three sons: Abram, Nahor, and Haran. Haran died after having a son, Lot. Now Abram took Sarai as his wife.

Lech Lecha לך לך

GENESIS 12:1-17:27

CAST
GOD
ABRAM/ABRAHAM
SARAI/SARAH
NARRATOR
PHARAOH
SHEPHERD 1
SHEPHERD 2
LOT
KING
MESSENGER

GOD: Abram, are you listening?

ABRAM: Yes, Holy One, Blessed Be You, I was just looking for a new tent. Now that our nephew Lot is living with us, my wife and I need more space.

GOD: Get yourself out of this country. Leave your family and your father's house, and go to a land that I will show you.

ABRAM: What? You want me to just pick up and leave everyone I know? Where am I supposed to go?

GOD: To a place that I will show you.

ABRAM: All right, I get the message.

GOD: In return, I will make you a great nation and I will make of you a great people.

SARAI: So, nu? Did you find a new tent?

ABRAM: Yes, I did. But . . Sarai, there are a few problems.

SARAI: Wonderful, where is it?

ABRAM: I don't know.

SARAI: What does it look like?

ABRAM: I don't know.

SARAI: Who is your real estate agent?

ABRAM: This agent is the very best, with connections all over the world.

SARAI: Feh! Who cares about the world? I want a two-bedroom tent right here in the suburbs. Who ever heard of such a deal? You bought a tent, but you don't know what it looks like or where it is? We are not paying a commission!

ABRAM: This is what God has commanded.

NARRATOR: And Abram took Sarai his wife, and Lot his brother's son, and all the substance that they had gathered, and they went forth to the land of Canaan.

GOD: This is the land that I will give you. How do you like it?

ABRAM: It's nice! Why Canaan?

GOD: Why not? It has ocean, beaches, mountains, and it's centrally located.

* * *

NARRATOR: There was famine in the land, and Abram went down to Egypt to dwell there.

ABRAM: Sarai, you are a beautiful woman.

SARAI: Thank you, Abram. A woman likes to hear that type of thing.

ABRAM: So, I want you to wear a paper bag over your head.

SARAI: What? I thought you said I was pretty!

ABRAM: If the Egyptians see you, they'll kill me and take you away. Maybe a paper bag is too drastic. I've got it. We'll say that we are sister and brother.

NARRATOR: The Egyptians saw Sarai. They saw how beautiful she was. They brought her to the Pharaoh, and she was taken into the palace. Abram was given sheep, oxen, slaves, donkeys, and camels. But God sent plagues to Pharaoh's house because Sarai was Abram's wife.

PHARAOH: Abram, why didn't you tell me Sarai was your wife?

ABRAM: You would have killed me and taken her.

PHARAOH: Maybe so. Why didn't you just put a paper bag over her head? That's what everyone else does when they visit Egypt with beautiful wives. Now, be gone! Get out of here! Go away!

NARRATOR: From Egypt, Abram went up into the Negev with his wife and all he possessed, and with Lot. But problems soon occurred.

SHEPHERD 1: Hey, we were at the water well first. Abram must have his sheep watered.

SHEPHERD 2: Lot needs his sheep watered, too. This land isn't big enough for the both of them.

SHEPHERD 1: Then move!

SHEPHERD 2: You move. Hey, you almost hit me with that sheep!

LOT: Look, Uncle Abe. Our shepherds are playing some new game.

ABRAM: What do you mean?

LOT: They're throwing sheep at each other.

ABRAM: Lot, I think they're trying to kill each other.

LOT: Wow, that's a dangerous game!

ABRAM: Let there be no strife between you and me, between your sheprds and mine, for we are relatives. Let us separate. If you go north, I'll go south, if you go south . . .

LOT: Okay, I'll take the plains of Jordan.

NARRATOR: And so they parted. Lot journeyed eastward. And God came to Abram.

GOD: Abram, look to the north, the south, the east, and the west. All this land will be yours. I shall make your offspring as numerous as the dust of the earth.

ABRAM: One, two, three, four, five . . .

GOD: What are you doing?

ABRAM: I'm counting the dust to get a rough estimate.

GOD: It's a whole lot, Abram. Trust me.

* * *

NARRATOR: Presenting the world's first melodrama. A war takes place between five kings and four kings. And the alliance of five kings, which included Sodom and Gomorrah, lost. They took many people hostage, including Lot.

LOT: Woe is me! Help! Help! Someone please save me!

KING: Never. You will be a slave forever.

MESSENGER: Telegram for Abram.

ABRAM: Yes?

MESSENGER: "Woe is me! Help! Help! Someone please save me! Stop." That will be twenty shekels.

ABRAM: Hark! My nephew Lot is in trouble. Round up the posse! I will save him!

LOT: Help! Help!

KING: You'll never get away. Abram will not find you.

ABRAM: Wrong! Evil king, release my nephew and all those you have captured.

KING: Or what?

ABRAM: The three hundred and eighteen men behind me will descend on you.

KING: I see your point. I was just thinking of letting everyone go anyway.

LOT: My hero!

NARRATOR: And Abram brought back all the captured possessions. He brought back Lot and his possessions, and the women, and the rest of the people.

* * *

GOD: Abram, why are you pouting?

ABRAM: I have no children. I'm getting old.

GOD: I told you that I shall make you as numerous as the stars. Your children will be strangers in a strange land, and they shall be slaves and oppressed for 400 years. But they shall go free with great wealth, and I will punish the nation that they serve.

ABRAM: Sarai, the Almighty has promised to make of me a great nation.

SARAI: Wonderful. Did you lock up the camels?

ABRAM: Yes. Listen, don't you believe me?

SARAI: I'm old. If you are planning on having a great nation, it won't be by me. But, as a gift, I will give you my handmaiden, Hagar.

* * *

NARRATOR: Hagar became pregnant with Abram's child.

SARAI: Abram, I want her out. She thinks she is a queen now that she is pregnant. I want her out of here!

ABRAM: Sarai, have pity. She's pregnant. She will bear my first child. However, it is up to you what happens to her — just remember that. I know you will have sympathy for her feelings.

SARAI: Hagar, come here a moment. Hagar, I can understand how you feel bearing your master's first child. Get out of the tent. I've packed your bags. You have ten minutes.

NARRATOR: Hagar fled to the wilderness. But an angel appeared to her and told her to return to Sarai and submit to her harsh treatment. In return, Hagar was to have a son who would father a great people. Hagar returned. She came back to Sarai and bore Ishmael, the father of Arab nations.

GOD: Abram, I will make of you a multitude of nations. You shall no longer be called Abram, but Abraham, which means father of nations.

ABRAHAM: First you give me a new home. Now you give me a new name.

GOD: And to show you how generous I am, I will also give you a new child by Sarai.

ABRAHAM: Ha! I am 99 years old and Sarai is 90. It's physically impossible!

GOD: That's why you are man and I am God. Abraham, listen closely. Sarah will have a child. You'll name him Isaac. I will maintain the covenant with him. Ishmael will also be blessed, but Isaac is the one I'll do business with when you are gone.

ABRAHAM: You just called my wife Sarah.

GOD: That's right. I am changing her name, too. She will be known as Sarah, for she is blessed.

ABRAHAM: This is a lot of changes! First a new home, now new names and a new child. I'm going to father great nations. I'd like this covenant in writing, if you don't mind.

GOD: I agree. You and your offspring through the ages will keep my covenant. They shall believe and have faith in me. I will be their shield. Every male among you shall be circumcised. That shall be the sign of the covenant between you and Me. And throughout the generations, every male among you shall be circumcised at the age of eight days.

ABRAHAM: Circumcised? All I said was that I wanted it in writing. I'll settle for a verbal agreement. Besides, all You did for Noah was make a rainbow. He didn't have to be circumcised.

GOD: My standards are getting tougher. No *brit milah*, no great nation.

ABRAHAM: Sarah will never believe this.

GOD: Have faith in me, Abraham.

NARRATOR: Thus, Abraham and his son Ishmael were circumcised on that very day, and all his household with him.

Vayera

ויּרא

GENESIS 18:1-22:24

CAST
ANGEL 1
ANGEL 2
ANGEL 3
ABRAHAM
SARAH
GOD
NARRATOR
LOT
WIFE
MAID
ISAAC

ANGEL 1: Boy, is it hot out here! How did we end up with this assignment?

ANGEL 2: I don't know, but someone up there is probably enjoying this.

ANGEL 3: I always thought of myself as a pretty good angel. When the Boss called me in and said, "I have a mission for you," I was thinking of the Riviera or Las Vegas. I didn't expect the Canaan desert.

ANGEL 1: Look, there's a tent up ahead.

ANGEL 2: Someone's standing in front of it.

ANGEL 3: He's coming toward us. It looks like Abraham.

ANGEL 1: He's one of God's favorites.

ABRAHAM: Hello, strangers! Welcome to my tent. It's my pleasure to serve you. You look like you need some water, a foot bath, some bread, and a tree to recline under. What do you say? Sarah, three measures of flour, one choice calf, and some milk, please.

SARAH: Is that for here or to go?

ABRAHAM: For here or to go, fellas?

ANGEL 3: For here.

ABRAHAM: Well, sit under any tree you like.

ANGEL 1: We would like to give you something for your kindness.

ABRAHAM: Please don't   it's on the tent.

ANGEL 2: Abraham, I will return to you next year when your wife Sarah will have a son.

SARAH: I heard that. Ha! As a matter of fact, double ha! Look at me. How old do you think I am? Don't answer. I am pretty old, and we'll keep it at that. Now listen, Sir. You're a grown man and I don't have to tell you that I am past the baby making years.

GOD: Abraham, why did Sarah laugh and question having a child at her age? Let me remind you that for God, nothing is impossible.

* * *

NARRATOR: And the men set out from there, and looked down toward Sodom.

GOD: Abraham, I was going to hide this from you, but I decided not to.

ABRAHAM: Oh, good. I love secrets.

GOD: The reason I am telling you this is because you are going to become a great nation, and you should be aware of how to guide people. The outrage of Sodom and Gomorrah is so great and so serious, I will destroy them.

ABRAHAM: You're angry.

GOD: How could you tell?

ABRAHAM: You should consider this: Will you sweep away the innocent with the evil? What if there were fifty innocent people in the city? Wouldn't you forgive the place for their sake?

GOD: I am just. For fifty people, I would forgive them all. But Abraham, this is a very bad city. There are not fifty good people around.

ABRAHAM: Would you save the city if there were forty-five good people?

GOD: Yes.

ABRAHAM: If there were forty? thirty?

GOD: Yes.

ABRAHAM: Twenty?

GOD: Yes.

ABRAHAM: Ten?

GOD: Even if there were ten. But there aren't.

ABRAHAM: Wow. That must be some kind of wicked place! What goes on there?

GOD: You don't want to know.

* * *

NARRATOR: And two angels arrived in Sodom in the evening, as Lot was sitting in the gate of Sodom.

ANGEL 1: Who are we looking for?

ANGEL 2: The guy's name is Lot. He's Abraham's nephew.

ANGEL 1: What does he look like?

ANGEL 2: How should I know?

LOT: Gentlemen, please turn aside. Spend the night here. You'll be safe. You'll get some water. You'll bathe your feet. Maybe some food will help.

ANGEL 1: You sound just like someone we met earlier today. Do you know Abraham who lives in Mamre?

LOT: He's my uncle.

ANGEL 2: Thank goodness we found you! Have we got some news for you!

ANGEL 1: This town isn't so bad.

LOT: Are you kidding? I've got double locks on the door and I never go out at night without a spear. This place is crazy.

ANGEL 1: What's that noise outside?

LOT: I'll go check.

NARRATOR: The townspeople of Sodom, young and old — all the people to the last person — gathered around the

24

house. They shouted to Lot: Where are the men who came to you tonight? Bring them outside so we can deal with them.

LOT: Please, these people are my guests. Take my daughters, but don't hurt them.

ANGEL 2: Lot, get inside. They'll kill you. What a rough place! This calls for Heavenly Emergency Plan Number 178.

NARRATOR: The people who were at the entrance of the house, young and old, were struck with blinding light, so they couldn't find the door.

ANGEL 2: Works every time. Listen, Lot, God is about to destroy this city. Take your wife and two daughters and run for the hills. This place is going to be flattened. It won't be here tomorrow.

NARRATOR: So the men grabbed hold of Lot's hand, the hand of his wife, and the hands of his two daughters, and directed them outside the city.

LOT: You don't have to be so pushy.

ANGEL 1: Get moving — this place is going to blow! And whatever you do, do not look back. Now, get going!

LOT: The ground is shaking! Run!

ANGEL 2: 5, 4, 3, 2, 1 . . . Shalom Sodom and Gomorrah!

WIFE: Honey, I have to go back. I forgot my purse.

LOT: No, no — don't turn around!

NARRATOR: Lot's wife looked back, and thereupon she turned into a pillar of salt.

* * *

NARRATOR: And Abraham journeyed to the region of the Negev.

ABRAHAM: Sarah, you are a beautiful woman.

SARAH: Abraham, not that again. Do you want me to tell them you're my brother?

ABRAHAM: King Abimelech might get mad. I am sure things will work out.

NARRATOR: As usual, they didn't. Abimelech took Sarah as a wife. God appeared to him in a dream and said:

GOD: That is Abraham's wife. Give her back or I will make sure you die.

NARRATOR: And Abimelech returned Sarah to Abraham, and gave him gifts of sheep, oxen, and servants. He also gave Abraham land on which to settle.

* * *

MAID: Mazel tov, everybody! Sarah has had a baby boy!

SARAH: It is just as God promised.

MAID: What are you going to name him?

SARAH: Isaac, which means laughter, because I laughed when God promised me a child.

ABRAHAM: Isaac has been circumcised. Eight days old and so cute!

NARRATOR: And when Isaac was two, Abraham held a great feast.

SARAH: Abraham, I would like to talk with you.

ABRAHAM: It's a party. Can't it wait?

SARAH: Ishmael is playing with Isaac.

ABRAHAM: Isn't that sweet?

SARAH: Look into my eyes. Does it look like I think it's sweet?

ABRAHAM: If looks could kill, I'd be dead. What do you want? Anything you want I'll do.

SARAH: Get rid of them. I want them out. Ishmael will be a bad influence. He will not share the inheritance.

ABRAHAM: That's harsh. He is my son also.

GOD: May I interject a few words? Do what Sarah says, because your offspring will be continued through Isaac. I'll take care of Hagar and Ishmael.

NARRATOR: Early the next morning, Abraham took bread and a skin of water and gave them to Hagar. She wandered in the wilderness. When the water was gone, she left her child in the bushes, for she did not wish to see her child die. She moved off and burst into tears.

ANGEL 3: Hi. How are you? That's a dumb question. Listen, we're really sorry about this foul-up. So look what presents we have for you. Come here, Ishmael. He's a nice looking kid. Tell you what: We'll make him a great nation. I bet you'll like that. And watch this — it's my favorite miracle. Look, a well of water! Now go, Hagar. Dry those eyes. God is with you.

* * *

NARRATOR: The servants of Abimelech and Abraham were quarreling, and so the King and Abraham made a pact.

Abraham dug a well and gave Abimelech seven sheep as proof of their agreement. Hence, the place was called Beersheva.

GOD: Abraham, I have a test for you.

ABRAHAM: Let me get a pencil.

GOD: Not exactly what I had in mind. Take your son, your favorite son, the one you love, Isaac, and go to the land of Moriah and offer him there as a sacrifice on one of the mountains which I will show you.

NARRATOR: So early the next morning, Abraham saddled his donkey and took with him Isaac and two servants. They traveled for three days.

ABRAHAM: Stay here with the donkeys. Isaac and I will go the rest of the way ourselves.

ISAAC: Father, you said we're going to sacrifice something, right?

ABRAHAM: That's right.

ISAAC: Well, silly us. We forgot an animal. All we have is the knife and wood.

ABRAHAM: Son, this is hard to say. You are the sacrifice.

ISAAC: Me? You're kidding. Look how skinny I am! I'd be terrible as a sacrifice, Dad. I don't mind going back down the mountain for a sheep, really.

ABRAHAM: This is what God commanded.

ISAAC: Maybe you misunderstood. It's a possibility. You are shaking your head no. You're picking me up. You're putting me on the altar. You're lifting the knife. You're really not kidding! Ohhh . . .

28

ANGEL 3: Abraham! Abraham! Boy, I got here just in time. You passed the test, for I know that you fear God since you have not withheld your favorite son from Me. There's a ram caught in the bushes. Sacrifice it instead.

ISAAC: Am I glad to see you!

ANGEL 3: God will bless you and make you as numerous as the stars, and the sands on the seashores. For you obeyed my command.

Chayay Sarah חיי שרה

GENESIS 23:1-25:18

CAST
NARRATOR
ABRAHAM
MAN
EPHRON
VOICE
ELIEZER
REBEKAH
LABAN

NARRATOR: Sarah's lifetime came to one hundred and twenty and seven years. Sarah died in Kiriat Arba — now Hebron — in the land of Canaan.

ABRAHAM: Neighbors, I am a stranger among you. Sell me a burial site for Sarah.

MAN: Abraham, you are known as a favorite of God. Bury Sarah wherever you like.

ABRAHAM: Could you talk to Ephron the son of Zohar? I would like to buy the Cave Of Machpelah. I'll buy it for the full price.

EPHRON: I can't beat a deal like that. I'm sorry, I couldn't help overhearing my name.

MAN: Ephron!

EPHRON: Okay, you can have the cave for free.

ABRAHAM: I can't do that. I want to pay the price.

EPHRON: Since I can't seem to convince you otherwise, how about 400 silver shekels? After all, we're friends!

ABRAHAM: Ephron, you are an expensive friend, but it's a deal.

NARRATOR: Then Abraham buried his wife Sarah in the cave of the field of Machpelah, facing Mamre, in the land of Canaan.

* * *

VOICE: Good afternoon, Eliezer, faithful servant of Abraham. Abraham is getting old, and is worried about Isaac not being married. He does not want Isaac to marry a Canaanite. Instead, he wishes a woman from his home country. Your mission is to take ten camels, travel back to the land of Abraham's family, and bring back a wife for Isaac. If the woman refuses to come and wants Isaac to go there, the answer is no. Bring her here. As usual, if you try hard and nothing goes right, you are excused from the mission.

ELIEZER: Pardon me. Where am I?

MAN: You are in the city of Nahor in the land of the Arameans.

ELIEZER: Aram! I made it! Now what do I do? I've got it. I'll make a sign. The first girl that says to me as I sit by the well, "Drink, and I will also draw water for your camels" is to be the wife for Isaac. After all, he's not here to help so I don't think he can afford to be picky.

REBEKAH: Excuse me, I'd like to draw some water and you are blocking my way.

ELIEZER: Oh, pardon me. I've been on the road with ten camels for I don't know how long. I don't know where to park in this city. Has anyone ever told you that you are beautiful?

31

REBEKAH: Well, if you count Ari down at the beggar's market, twenty-five people have mentioned it today. Being so kvetchy, you must be thirsty. Let me pour you some water. Here, drink, and I will also draw water for your camels.

ELIEZER: Bingo! She shoots, she scores! Congratulations, you have just won first prize!

REBEKAH: I did? I won?

ELIEZER: That's right.

REBEKAH: What's the prize? A new silk wardrobe?

ELIEZER: Better than that. It's an all expense paid trip to Canaan!

REBEKAH: Canaan?

ELIEZER: And there you will become the bride of Isaac!

REBEKAH: Isaac? Who is Isaac?

ELIEZER: No more questions. Whose daughter are you?

REBEKAH: I am the daughter of Bethuel, the son of Milcah.

ELIEZER: Double Bingo! You are relatives of Abraham. Let's go find the head of the household.

NARRATOR: Laban, Rebekah's older brother, greeted Eliezer and welcomed him to their home. Then food was set down and Eliezer began his tale.

ELIEZER: So that's the way it was. Can you believe all the coincidences?

LABAN: It is God's will. Take Rebekah for a wife to your master's son. But let her stay here ten more days.

32

ELIEZER: I'm sorry. I am running so late right now. I have to get back to Canaan. Will you let her come now?

LABAN: Will you go with this man?

REBEKAH: I will.

NARRATOR: Then Rebekah and her maids arose, mounted the camels, and followed the man. So the servant took Rebekah and went his way.

REBEKAH: Are we there yet?

ELIEZER: Rebekah, we are almost home.

REBEKAH: Who is that beautiful man coming toward us? Hold me back! I am in love! He is really handsome. Eliezer, introduce us.

ELIEZER: That is Isaac, my master.

REBEKAH: Dear me! Where is my veil? Quick girls, cover my face!

ISAAC: Hello, my name is Isaac. I'm your future husband. Has anyone ever told you that you're beautiful?

REBEKAH: If you count Eliezer by the well, twenty-six people have told me that in the recent past. Coming from you, though, oh wow!

NARRATOR: Isaac then brought her into the tent of his mother Sarah, and he took Rebekah as his wife. Isaac loved her and thus found comfort after his mother's death. Abraham married again and had many more children, but all that he owned went to Isaac. And Abraham died at the age of one hundred and seventy-five. Isaac and Ishmael buried him in the Cave of Machpelah beside Sarah.

Toledot

CAST
NARRATOR
REBEKAH
GOD
JACOB
ESAU
ISAAC

NARRATOR: Let's do a summary of the whole story up 'til now. Abraham begot Isaac, and Isaac married Rebekah, and Rebekah couldn't have children for a while. They prayed to God and Rebekah became pregnant. Twins. And the children struggled within her and so she asked God . . .

REBEKAH: God, could you please tell me what is happening? I feel like there's a wrestling match going on inside me!

GOD: Rebekah, you're going to have twins. Two nations are in your womb.

REBEKAH: All I wanted was to have a little baby. You're giving me two nations to lug around. Don't You think You got carried away?

GOD: There is more.

REBEKAH: What are You saying? I'm going to have triplets? There's a third one in there acting as referee?

GOD: Relax, Rebekah. Just two. But there is more to the prediction. Once the peoples are separated from you, one will be stronger than the other, and the elder will serve the younger.

NARRATOR: Meanwhile, inside Rebekah . . .

JACOB: I want to go out first.

ESAU: Forget it, brother dear. I am getting out first.

JACOB: Oh yeah? Take this!

REBEKAH: They're fighting again.

NARRATOR: And finally the day arrived when the twins were to be born.

ESAU: Hey, brother. Look over there. Can you see it?

JACOB: What? Where is it?

ESAU: So long, pal!

NARRATOR: And the first one out was covered with a hairy mantle, and they named him Esau.

JACOB: Hey, you tricked me! Come back here right now!

ESAU: Let go of my heel!

NARRATOR: And after that came forth his brother, and his hand was holding Esau's heel, and so they called him Jacob. As they grew up, Esau became a hunter, while Jacob was a quiet man who dwelled in tents. Isaac favored Esau and Rebekah favored Jacob. One day . . .

ESAU: Boy, what a day! I must have hunted down an entire herd. I'm home, everybody!

JACOB: Oh, great. What has Mr. Macho Man killed for his daddy today?

ESAU: Knock it off, Jake. What are you cooking?

JACOB: Some stew, and it's not for you.

ESAU: Is it for dearest mommy? Come on, Jake, I'm starving!

JACOB: What will you give me?

ESAU: How about my hunting knife?

JACOB: How about selling me your birthright?

ESAU: Jake, I'm starving. If you want the birthright, it's yours.

JACOB: Have all the food you want.

* * *

GOD: Hello, Isaac, how are you?

ISAAC: God, is that You?

GOD: None other. We haven't stayed in touch as much as I would have liked. What's happening in Canaan from your point of view?

ISAAC: After the great famine, we moved to the land of the Philistines. Rebekah didn't want to go. She didn't want the boys changing neighborhoods and schools, but things were drying up. After a little run-in with Abimelech we made peace, and I'm pretty well established now in Beersheva.

GOD: So, nu? Where's the altar?

ISAAC: Oops.

GOD: Isaac, slow down. You're doing fine.

ISAAC: I'll have the altar built in a few minutes.

GOD: I am the God of Abraham, your father. Fear not, for I am with you, and will bless you, and will multiply your seed for the sake of my servant Abraham.

* * *

NARRATOR: And it came to pass when Isaac was old and his eyes were dim and he could not see . . .

ISAAC: Esau, where are you? You're such a great son.

ESAU: Dad, I'm the greatest son in the whole world.

ISAAC: I'm getting old. Go out there and hunt me some food. After you've done that, I shall bless you.

ESAU: Bless me? That means I get the inheritance! I'll be back before you can say "Connie Canaan can't come camel riding."

NARRATOR: Esau went out to the fields. Rebekah, meanwhile, called to Jacob.

REBEKAH: Jacob, I want you to go out to the flock and get two baby goats.

JACOB: We're having goat chops for dinner? I thought you said it was going to be leftovers tonight.

REBEKAH: Esau went out to kill some food to prepare in order to receive Isaac's blessing. I want you to get the blessing.

JACOB: Mother, that's not nice. You're telling me to deceive my father. Are you actually saying that I should steal Esau's blessing? Do you think that I would do that? Do you think I would conspire against both my father and my brother just for the inheritance of Canaan?

REBEKAH: I think so.

JACOB: I'll be back in a second.

REBEKAH: I'll boil the water.

JACOB: Hair!

REBEKAH: What?

JACOB: I forgot — hair. Esau has lots of hair. When Dad touches me, he'll know it's not Esau. If he figures it out, he'll curse me!

REBEKAH: If he curses you, it's on my head.

JACOB: Oh. That's different.

NARRATOR: And Rebekah made delicious food, and put Esau's finest clothes on Jacob. Around his neck and hands, she put the skins of goats. And Jacob went into the tent.

JACOB: Hello, father. I'm back with the food you asked for.

ISAAC: Who is that?

JACOB: I am Esau, your oldest son. Don't you remember?

ISAAC: Of course. But how did you catch the food so quickly?

JACOB: Funny that you should ask. I, uh, this . . . uh, this deer just ran out in front of me and just seemed to be saying, "Here I am! A delicious dinner for your Daddy!"

ISAAC: Something fishy is going on. Draw near. I wish to touch you to see if you are indeed Esau.

JACOB: Hey, Dad, come on, stop! You're tickling me.

ISAAC: You have the hands of Esau, but the voice of Jacob.

JACOB: I've got a cold. *(Cough.)*

ISAAC: Draw near and I shall bless you.

NARRATOR: And Isaac blessed Jacob saying: Let peoples serve thee. Be lord over your brothers. Let your mother's sons bow to you. Cursed be those who curse you, and blessed be those who bless you.

REBEKAH: Pssst, Jacob! Hurry up! Esau is coming.

JACOB: Dad, thanks for the blessing. I've got to go.

ESAU: I'm home, Dad! I hope you're hungry.

ISAAC: I am stuffed.

ESAU: I thought you told me to get some food for you!

ISAAC: Who are you?

ESAU: I'm Esau, remember? Your favorite little hunter. Let's eat and then you'll bless me.

ISAAC: Oh no, I blessed the wrong son. Jacob tricked me!

ESAU: Bless me, too.

ISAAC: I can't. It's impossible to go back on my word.

ESAU: Please, I go back on my word all the time. What did you bless him with?

ISAAC: Everything! He got everything. By the sword shall you live, and you shall serve him.

ESAU: That little twerp. He has tricked me twice. I'll kill him!

ISAAC: That's a bit extreme.

ESAU: You're right. Death is too nice. I'll torture him first.

REBEKAH: Jacob, come here. Esau found out.

JACOB: How is he taking it?

REBEKAH: He'll feel better after he has killed you.

JACOB: Kill me? He wouldn't do that.

ESAU: Where is he? I am going to massacre him!

JACOB: Maybe he is a little bit upset. What do I do?

REBEKAH: You're going to Uncle Laban's house. I've packed your bags. Don't forget to change your tunic every day. Wash in the river. Write often. Here's the address. Stay there until Esau cools down.

JACOB: That could be 20 years.

REBEKAH: Try not to think of it that way.

NARRATOR: And Isaac called Jacob in and blessed him.

ISAAC: It's probably good that you are going to Uncle Laban's. Your mother and I don't want you marrying a Canaanite woman anyway. You must stick with your own kind. May God bless you.

ESAU: Where is my deeaaar brother?

ISAAC: Have a nice trip!

JACOB: I'm leaving right now.

Vayaytze

GENESIS 28:10-32:3

CAST
JACOB
ANGEL 1
ANGEL 2
ANGEL 3
GOD
NARRATOR
SHEPHERD
RACHEL
PERSON
LEAH
LABAN

JACOB: It's a long way to Uncle Laban's, it's a long way to go. I *had* to steal the birthright. I *had* to steal my brother's blessing. Now look what's happened! He's still home with Isaac and Rebekah, and I'm on the run. This running has got me pooped. I think I'll bunk for the night. Great — a nice bed of dirt and a rock for a pillow.

ANGEL 1: Going up.

ANGEL 2: Going down.

ANGEL 3: Don't push! There's room for everyone.

JACOB: What's going on? Am I dreaming?

ANGEL 1: Dreaming? No, I doubt it. You see, this is a ladder and we are angels. Some of us are punching in to do some business here, and some of us are punching out and going home. Are you coming or going?

41

JACOB: Huh? I don't understand.

ANGEL 3: You're not an angel, are you?

JACOB: No.

ANGEL 2: Big mistake! I thought you checked out the area before lowering the ladder.

ANGEL 1: I did. I was going to move it when I saw him sleeping, but the Boss told me to leave it where it was.

ANGEL 2: The Boss told you that? Hark! Surprise inspection, everyone. Do you hear that? It's the Boss, Numero Uno . . .

JACOB: To whom am I talking, please?

GOD: You are speaking to the Almighty.

JACOB: Oh, my God!

GOD: That's right. You catch on fast. Listen, son, I only have a few minutes. I have known both your father and grandfather, and I think it's time I let you in on a little agreement we've made. All of this land is going to be yours. I will make your offspring numerous and will protect you. Well, I've enjoyed our little talk. And Jacob — put the rock back where you found it.

JACOB: Wow, God was in this place and I, I did not know it! Truly I have been blessed. This is the gateway to heaven.

NARRATOR: And Jacob took the stone that had been under his head, and set it as an altar, and placed oil upon it. He named the site Bethel, meaning "Home of God." And he resumed his journey, and came to the land of the Easterners, and there before his eyes was a well.

* * *

JACOB: Excuse me, do you know the way to Laban's house?

SHEPHERD: Sure do. Oh, here comes his daughter, with the sheep.

JACOB: Wow! She's gorgeous!

SHEPHERD: Three times Miss Mesopotamia.

JACOB: Is she married?

SHEPHERD: Nope. Laban won't let her marry until her older sister Leah gets hitched.

JACOB: What's Leah like?

SHEPHERD: Put it this way, she has a nice personality.

JACOB: Hi, my name is Jacob and I am your cousin.
My mother, your Aunt Rebekah, sent me here to stay with Uncle Laban.

RACHEL: It's nice to meet you. I'll take you to the tent.

NARRATOR: And Jacob stayed with Laban a month, and Laban said to Jacob: Just because you're my kinsman, should you serve me for nothing? And it was agreed that Jacob would work for seven years to marry Rachel. And the years went like days because of Jacob's love for her.

SHEPHERD: Jacob, we're ready for you.

PERSON: Quiet, everyone! We're starting the wedding. Gershon, get the camel out of here! Shhhhh. Here's the bride. That is some dress, and look at that veil! Can you see where you're going? Hey, someone get the bride; she just walked out of the tent! I pronounce you husband and wife. Be fruitful and multiply.

JACOB: Rachel, time to wake up. Rachel? Hey, you're not Rachel!

LEAH: Hi, Jacob. Surprise!

JACOB: Leah, what are you doing here? Where did Rachel go?

LEAH: You married me, Jacob. Not Rachel.

JACOB: No! I specifically worked seven years to marry Rachel. Does she know about this? I've been had! SEVEN YEARS!

LABAN: Our custom is that the older sister marries first. Tell you what I'm going to do: Work another seven years and you can marry Rachel, too.

JACOB: Seven MORE years?

LABAN: All right. To show that I'm a fair guy, I'll throw in a few sheep.

NARRATOR: And Jacob served Laban another seven years. And he married Rachel also; indeed, he loved Rachel more than Leah.

PERSON: Ladies and gentlemen — announcing the starting line-up of the House of Jacob. The coaches: Rachel, Leah and the handmaidens Bilhah and Zilpah. The sons of Leah: Reuven, Simon, Levi, Judah, Issachar, Zebulun, and daughter Dinah. The sons of the handmaidens: Dan, Asher, Gad, and Naphtali. And the son of Rachel: Joseph. What a team! You've done well, Jacob.

NARRATOR: Jacob labored six more years for his uncle Laban. Laban began to grow jealous of Jacob's wealth and success, and dealt with him dishonestly. Jacob grew restless and when Laban was away, Jacob gathered his wives and children and all the livestock and all the wealth he had amassed, and took off. When Laban came home, he grew angry and made chase.

LABAN: Jacob, this is Laban, I've got you now!

JACOB: Oh, hi. Did you get my note? I put it in your tent. Something came up suddenly.

LABAN: Knock it off. I was not going to do you harm. After all, is that any way to say goodbye? I didn't even get to say Shalom to the grandchildren. I was peeved! But last night God came to me in a dream and said . . .

GOD: Laban, stop right there. You have been terrible to Jacob. If you touch one hair on his head, you'll be in trouble.

LABAN: Well, in that case . . . have you seen a few of my household items that seem to have disappeared about the time you did?

JACOB: That does it. I worked for you for 20 years and never took any animals that belonged to you. If a sheep was lost, I paid for it. Scorching heat burned me by day and frost chilled me at night. I had to work 14 years to marry your daughters after you pulled a fast one. Six more years I worked for the flocks, and you kept changing the wages. If it hadn't been for God's guidance, I'd be empty-handed right now. Have you got *chutzpah!* What are you missing? Some bobby pins? A jacket? Some loose change? A quart of milk?

LABAN: Jacob, Jacob. You're getting emotional.

JACOB: Emotional? Emotional? I am angry! I am very angry!

LABAN: Tell ya what. Let's make a pact. We'll make up. I think it will work as long as we stay out of each other's sight.

NARRATOR: And Laban said to Jacob: Here is a mound and here is a pillar that I have set up between us. This mound and pillar are to be witness that I shall not cross it with hostile intent, nor shall you. And they swore by God and offered sacrifices. In the morning, Laban kissed his daughters and grandchildren and bid them farewell.

Vayishlach

וישלח

CAST
NARRATOR
JACOB
SERVANT 1
SERVANT 2
COHEN
ANNOUNCER
ANGEL
SERVANT 3
ESAU
GOD

NARRATOR: When we last left our story, Jacob was returning to the land of Canaan after a 20 year absence. With him were his two wives and his two handmaidens, his eleven sons, one daughter, all of his servants, and a heap of cattle and sheep.

JACOB: All right, fellas. Here is a letter to my brother Esau. It tells him that I did well in the land of our Uncle Laban, and that I bring him many gifts. Hopefully, he will have forgotten the little disagreement we had before I left.

SERVANT 1: What little disagreement was that, Sir?

JACOB: I, uh, stole his birthright and then disguised myself to receive his inheritance blessing from our father, Isaac.

SERVANT 1: Do you really think he will have forgotten?

JACOB: No, but let's not worry.

47

SERVANT 1: But Sir, Esau is known as a powerful warrior with bloodthirsty methods of destroying his enemies. He is feared as being merciless. A killer.

JACOB: Must you try so hard to cheer me up? Send the message.

* * *

NARRATOR: And the messengers returned to Jacob saying: We came to your brother Esau, and moreover he comes to meet you with 400 men.

JACOB: Hmmmm. I guess he's still a little sore. What shall I do? I have it. I will pray to God for help. Oh God of Abraham and Isaac, deliver me from Esau. Don't let him hurt me or my family. Oh, God . . . don't let him hurt the children. I'll do anything. And remember, You told me that my offspring will be as numerous as the sand of the sea? Please tell me You remember Your promise.

SERVANT 1: Are you all right, Sir?

JACOB: Of course I am. My whole life is crumbling. We may not be alive tomorrow. Do you have the gifts for Esau ready?

SERVANT 2: 200 she-goats, 20 he-goats, 200 ewes, 20 rams, and for good measure we threw in some camels, bulls, cows, and donkeys.

JACOB: Hopefully, Esau will see all these gifts and be pleased when I approach.

SERVANT 2: After what you did to him, stealing his birthright?

JACOB: I'm glad all of my servants are so comforting and encouraging!

NARRATOR: And Jacob arose that night, and he took his two wives and his two handmaidens and his eleven sons, and passed over the Jabbok River. He took them and sent them over the stream, and sent over that which he had. And Jacob was left alone.

JACOB: Who goes there?

COHEN: Ladies and gentlemen! Welcome to the Peniel Auditorium! Our timekeeper at the bell is the angel Michael. The doctor at ringside is Dr. Harvey Shapiro, and my name is Dave Cohen. The main event is scheduled for two hours, or curfew at dawn. In this corner is an angel of the Holy One. And in the opposite corner is the slightly bewildered Jacob. Are you ready to rumble?

ANNOUNCER: Man oh man alive. What a match! Jacob has the angel in a full Nelson. Ooh! And the angel flips his opponent over! The crowd is yelling for the Indian death lock.

ANGEL: Jacob, just throw the match. It's almost dawn and I have to go. This is only a second job. I'll give you twenty shekels.

JACOB: No way. I'm going for the title!

ANNOUNCER: The angel has touched the hollow of Jacob's thigh, and it looks like his thigh is hurt!

JACOB: Ow! Ow!

ANGEL: Jacob, let go of me. You can have the title. As a matter of fact, I shall give you a new name. It shall be "Israel," for you have striven with God and with men and have prevailed.

NARRATOR: And the sun rose and Jacob limped upon his thigh. That is why the children of Israel do not eat the meat of an animal's vein which is in the hollow of the thigh.

* * *

SERVANT 3: Jacob, you look like you've been in a fight. Have you already seen Esau?

JACOB: Esau?

SERVANT 3: He's right in front of us with his 400 men.

SERVANT 2: Don't look now, Sir, but he's riding right toward you.

JACOB: Esau! Hello.

ESAU: Jacob, relax. It's so good to see you!

NARRATOR: And Esau embraced Jacob and fell on his neck and kissed him and they both wept.

JACOB: It is so good to still be alive. Let me introduce you to my four wives and eleven sons.

ESAU: Hi, everyone. I'm your Uncle Esau. Jacob, I do not need your gifts. I have plenty.

JACOB: Please keep them as a sign of my gratitude.

ESAU: As you wish, my brother. Now that you have returned, come and make your home near me.

JACOB: You go on ahead, Esau. The women and children move so slowly, you know. I have a job offer in the neighborhood. I'll keep in touch.

* * *

GOD: Jacob, this is God.

JACOB: I am here.

GOD: Your name is Israel. It shall no longer be Jacob.

JACOB: You heard about the match?

GOD: You were great, Jacob. And now, be fruitful and multiply. A nation and a company of nations shall come of thee. The land that I gave to Abraham and Isaac, I shall give to you and your children.

NARRATOR: And Jacob built an altar there and called it Bethel. On the way to Ephrath, Rachel went into labor. She was in hard labor, but the midwife said, "Fear not for it is a son." The child was called Benjamin. And Rachel died. Jacob set up a pillar on the road to Ephrath as Rachel's grave, and it is there to this day.

ANNOUNCER: And later, Isaac died. He was 180 years old. And Esau and Jacob, his sons, buried him. Esau became the head of the Edomite nation and had lots and lots and lots of children.

Vayayshev

GENESIS 37:1-40:23

CAST
NARRATOR
JOSEPH
GAD
ZEBULUN
ASHER
REUVEN
JUDAH
NAPHTALI
DAN
LEVI
JACOB
SIMON
ISSACHAR
POTIPHAR
WIFE
CUPBEARER
BAKER

NARRATOR: Jacob settled in the land of Canaan, and lived there with his wives and children.

JOSEPH: Is it my turn to start talking?

NARRATOR: I haven't finished what I was saying.

JOSEPH: Well, hurry up. After all, I'm the star of this story.

NARRATOR: Now Israel loved Joseph best of all his sons. At age seventeen, Joseph tended the flock with his brothers. He brought bad reports of them to his father.

JOSEPH: I am observing Zebulun and Gad. They are sitting down. This is their third water break this week. Asher is joining them.

GAD: Is he watching us again?

ZEBULUN: Yes, your favorite little spy is writing up some more reports on his "terrible" brothers.

ASHER: Last week, he told Dad I was irresponsible because when I was chasing a lamb I fell down and stubbed my toe. Instead of getting up to keep running, I stopped to put some cold water on it.

GAD: Why Asher! What a naughty son you are.

JOSEPH: They continue to talk. I shall attempt to get closer to hear what they are saying.

GAD: He's crawling over here. I'm beginning to hate that little creep.

NARRATOR: Aside from spying, Joseph took up dreaming as a hobby. That's like TV without the electronics.

JOSEPH: Hello, my brothers. Isn't it nice to see me? Look at this coat that our father has given me.

REUVEN: It's really nice, Joseph.

JOSEPH: It's more than nice. It's fabulous!

JUDAH: Joseph, have I told you today how much I love you?

JOSEPH: No, Judah, you haven't.

JUDAH: Good!

JOSEPH: Besides wanting to show you my coat, I had a dream last night. Who wants to hear it?

NAPHTALI: Nobody!

GAD: Not me.

DAN: Who cares?

JOSEPH: Great. We were binding sheaves in the field, and suddenly my sheaf stood up and yours gathered around and bowed to mine.

LEVI: Does that mean that you're going to rule over us?

JOSEPH: I'm not suggesting anything. After all, it's merely a dream. Of course, my dreams always seem to come true.

JUDAH: Joseph, have I told you yet this year that I love you?

JOSEPH: No.

JUDAH: Good!

JOSEPH: I had another dream as well. Who wants to hear it?

DAN: The Ishmaelites want to hear it.

JOSEPH: They live twenty miles away.

GAD: If you hurry, you can reach their tents by sundown.

JOSEPH: Here's my dream: The sun, the moon and eleven stars all bowed down to me.

NARRATOR: When Jacob heard this dream, he scolded Joseph.

JACOB: Are we, your father and mother and your brothers, to bow low before you?

JOSEPH: Dad, it was only a dream. I call 'em like I see 'em.

* * *

NARRATOR: One day, Joseph was sent by Jacob to help his brothers tend sheep in Shechem.

SIMON: Look who's coming — the dreamer. Let's beat him up.

LEVI: Let's break a few bones.

NAPHTALI: Better yet, let's tear him apart!

ASHER: That would be too nice. Let's torture him over a fire.

GAD: We could also let an accident happen to him.

REUVEN: Brothers, Joseph is a brat, but he is our brother. Let us not take his life.

NAPHTALI: Every party has a pooper — that's why we invited you.

ZEBULUN: All right, let's dump him in the pit instead.

ISSACHAR: Shhh. Here he comes. Joseph, right this way!

JOSEPH: It's about time I found you. I went to Shechem and you weren't there and some guy told me you were in Dothan. And . . . why are you looking at me like that? I don't like this. Hey, watch it! That's my coat. I just got it back from the cleaners. Careful! Now what? A pit! I'm not jumping in there. I'll sue. Help! Daddy, save me!

JUDAH: Look over there — Ishmaelites. Let's sell our dear little brother to them.

NARRATOR: And the brothers sold Joseph to the Ishmaelites for twenty shekels of silver.

* * *

REUVEN: Father, we have terrible news.

JACOB: What could be so bad?

REUVEN: Joseph is dead. Oh, Dad, it was terrible. There we were, coming back from tending sheep. Joseph, as usual, was telling jokes and was the center of attention.

GAD: We really loved that little fella.

REUVEN: Anyhow, this person-eating lion jumped out.

ZEBULUN: You can imagine how scared we all were!

REUVEN: But Joseph yelled, "Stand back, I'll protect you!" And the lion attacked him!

ISSACHAR: This is all that was left — a part of his coat

NARRATOR: Jacob mourned for many days, and nobody could comfort him. Meanwhile, Joseph was taken down to Egypt and sold to Potiphar, an important man in the Egyptian court.

* * *

POTIPHAR: Joseph, I like the way you work. From now on, you are chief servant in my house.

JOSEPH: Thanks, Mr. Potiphar. I'll do my best.

POTIPHAR: Take care of all of my household possessions . . . uh . . . except my wife.

WIFE: Joseph, come here to me.

JOSEPH: I can't do that. Mr. Potiphar would get upset.

WIFE: Don't be so stuffy. I won't bite. On second thought, maybe I will — you are so cute!

JOSEPH: Cute is one thing, but bad is another.

WIFE: I know. And I love being bad!

JOSEPH: Hey, let go of my coat! It's brand new. You're ripping the seams!

WIFE: Either you stay with me or I'll scream.

JOSEPH: Keep the coat — I'm getting out of here.

WIFE: HELP!!! Joseph just attacked me. HELP!!!

POTIPHAR: Joseph, you attacked my wife. You will go to jail for this.

JOSEPH: I'm innocent!

POTIPHAR: My wife disagrees.

JOSEPH: Does this mean I don't get any more free tickets to the camel races?

* * *

NARRATOR: So Joseph's master put him in prison. But while he was there, God was with Joseph. The chief jailer put Joseph in charge of all the prisoners.

CUPBEARER: Excuse me, are you Joseph?

JOSEPH: The one and only.

CUPBEARER: I had a bad dream last night. There were three branches on this vine that were barely budding. Suddenly they blossomed and I squeezed the grapes into wine for Pharaoh. What does it mean? I am so confused!

JOSEPH: The three branches stand for three days. In three days, Pharaoh will pardon you and you'll once again be his cupbearer.

BAKER: Joseph, as long as you're interpreting dreams so nicely, how about doing mine? There were three baskets on my head with food in them. Birds were eating from the top one. Does that mean in three days I will be free also?

JOSEPH: No, but guess again.

BAKER: In three days, I'll be free and Pharoah will make me a rich man.

JOSEPH: Wrong.

BAKER: I'll be free and rich and will own my own bakery shop, in three days?

JOSEPH: Actually, in three days you'll be dead.

BAKER: Thanks for being so cheery. How come the cupbearer gets to live?

JOSEPH: Hey, I only interpret dreams. But since it didn't turn out so well, I'm giving you a discount.

NARRATOR: And so it was that Pharaoh had a banquet, and he restored the cupbearer to his job. The baker he put to death.

CUPBEARER: Joseph, I'm packed and ready to go. Thanks for helping me.

JOSEPH: Please don't forget me. Mention me to Pharaoh. After all, I was a poor Hebrew that was sold into slavery. Maybe he'll do something for me.

CUPBEARER: Joseph, I won't forget. How could anybody forget you?

NARRATOR: But the cupbearer forgot him.

Mikaytz

מִקֵּץ

GENESIS 41:1-44:17

CAST
LIZ
NELLIE
PHARAOH
DOCTOR
CALLER
CUPBEARER
JOSEPH
NARRATOR
JACOB
REUVEN
SIMON
LEVI
JUDAH
ISSACHAR
GAD
EGYPTIAN

LIZ: Good evening, ladies and gentlemen. Liz Luxor here with tonight's top story, the mysterious nightmares of our great leader, the Pharaoh. We go now to the palace for a live interview with the king.

NELLIE: Thank you, Liz. Nellie Nile here with the great Pharaoh. Pharaoh, tell us about your dream.

PHARAOH: It was wild indeed. I saw these seven fat cows walking along the banks of the Nile.

NELLIE: Seven fat cows? Pardon me for laughing, but did you say cows?

PHARAOH: Yes, and these seven thin and very ugly cows came up out of the river and ate them. After eating, they still stayed skinny.

NELLIE: Fat cows? Thin cows? It's a puzzle. This is Nellie Nile. We'll be back with breaking news if the Pharaoh dreams again.

* * *

PHARAOH: AAAAHHH!!!!

DOCTOR: There he goes again. The dream.

PHARAOH: AAAAHHH!

DOCTOR: Pharaoh, wake up!

PHARAOH: I must know what that dream means!

CALLER: Hear ye! Hear ye! Interpret the Pharaoh's dream and win a cruise for two up the Nile on a reed raft!

CUPBEARER: Pharaoh, I just remembered a Hebrew lad who was good at interpreting dreams.

PHARAOH: Bring him to me.

JOSEPH: Oh, great Pharaoh, I am here.

PHARAOH: Interpret this dream correctly and you're a free man.

JOSEPH: And if I'm wrong?

PHARAOH: You're not going to want to be wrong.

JOSEPH: It is not I but God who will interpret your dreams.

PHARAOH: I keep dreaming about these cows. And then I see these seven healthy ears of grain growing on this stalk. Then these seven sickly ears sprout on the same stalk and eat the good ears. What does it all mean?

JOSEPH: It means that you will have seven years of bumper crops, followed by seven years of famine.

PHARAOH: WOW! A regular Sigmund Freud!

CUPBEARER: Sigmund who?

JOSEPH: My suggestion is that you find a man of ability who is wise. Set him over Egypt. There must be planning and rationing.

PHARAOH: Joseph, how about you?

JOSEPH: I humbly, humbly accept, oh great Pharaoh.

PHARAOH: I am Pharaoh, yet without you, no one shall lift up a hand or foot in all the land of Egypt.

NARRATOR: And Pharaoh put Joseph in charge of the land, and dressed him in fine clothes. Joseph wore a gold chain around his neck, and another new coat.

* * *

NARRATOR: Joseph was 30 years old when he entered Pharaoh's service. He was given Asenath as a wife and had two sons, Manasseh and Ephraim. Joseph traveled throughout the land collecting food in large quantities.

LIZ: Extra, extra! Read all about it! Egypt experiences seven years of abundant harvests!

JOSEPH: Well, that's it. If my predictions are right, here comes starvation city.

LIZ: Good evening, ladies and gentlemen, Liz Luxor here with tonight's top story. As predicted by Egypt's number two man, Joseph, we continue to see famine throughout the region. Due to planning ahead, Egypt's population is surviving.

However, many surrounding nations are now turning to Joseph to request food.

* * *

JACOB: My sons, we are starving. I want you to go to Egypt to buy some food.

REUVEN: Aren't there any other alternatives?

JACOB: Only Egypt has food. Go or we die.

REUVEN: I'll get the brothers ready to go.

NARRATOR: Thus the sons of Israel were among those who came to seek rations, for the famine extended to Canaan.

SIMON: Who is this guy that we have to talk to?

LEVI: His name is *Tzafnat-panayach*. It's Egyptian.

REUVEN: Come on. It's our turn to talk to Pharaoh's Number Two.

JOSEPH: *(In a whisper.)* Oh, my God!

SIMON: Excuse us, is something wrong, Sir?

NARRATOR: The brothers did not recognize Joseph, and so he acted as a stranger to them.

JOSEPH: Where are you from?

JUDAH: Canaan.

JOSEPH: I think you're spies.

ISSACHAR: Spies? Have the desert winds dried your mind?

JOSEPH: What?!

ISSACHAR: I mean, you are mistaken. We are twelve sons of a certain man in Canaan.

JOSEPH: Perhaps Canaan is teaching new math in their school system because I only count ten of you.

REUVEN: One is no more.

JOSEPH: I'm sorry. Losing a brother is terrible. You must have loved him dearly.

REUVEN: The other son is with our father.

JOSEPH: Spies! You're all spies. I will put you to a test. Bring back the other son or you shall never see my face again.

REUVEN: Benjamin is our youngest brother. Our father will not let him go.

JOSEPH: One of your brothers will stay with us, and the rest may return to Canaan. If you don't return, I'll know you are spies.

REUVEN: I told you this would happen.

GAD: What are you talking about, Reuven?

REUVEN: We should never have hurt Joseph. We're being punished for what we did to him. I told you guys to leave him alone.

SIMON: Quiet — suppose the Egyptian understands us?

JUDAH: No chance. He's been using an interpreter to talk to us.

JOSEPH: Enough talk! Take that man as prisoner. The rest of you may fill your sacks and return to your father.

SIMON: Me? Why me? I'm innocent! I've been a good person, except for the time I helped throw my brother into the pit. And there was that time I attacked Shechem . . . Oh, and . . . Hey, brothers, don't leave me here!

* * *

JACOB: My sons, you return from Egypt with food. Wonderful!

REUVEN: Father, we have this problem. The King's Number Two Man is holding Simon captive and won't let him go unless we return with Benjamin to show him proof that we are not spies.

JACOB: I've lost Joseph. I've lost Simon. And now you want me to lose Benjamin? Never!

NARRATOR: But the famine grew more severe.

JUDAH: Father, I must take Benjamin. You can hold me responsible for anything that happens.

* * *

NARRATOR: And so the brothers returned to Egypt. They presented gifts to Joseph, and showed him Benjamin. Joseph prepared a feast for them. While they ate, Joseph had his silver cup put in Benjamin's sack of food.

JOSEPH: So, how is your father?

LEVI: He's probably getting pretty hungry. We've got to be heading home. Thanks for getting things cleared up. It's good to see Simon again.

NARRATOR: And the brothers packed their animals and started off for Canaan when suddenly . . .

JUDAH: Hey, look. Here come the Egyptians. What could they want?

EGYPTIAN: Stop!

SIMON: That doesn't sound too friendly to me.

EGYPTIAN: So this is how you repay Egypt's generosity?

REUVEN: What did we do wrong?

EGYPTIAN: You stole the silver cup of our master!

ISSACHAR: We did not! You can kill anyone of us who you find with stolen possessions.

EGYPTIAN: Are you that sure of your innocence?

SIMON: Yes we are. You can kill whoever stole it.

EGYPTIAN: Nothing so far. We only have one more sack to check. This one.

REUVEN: You see? We wouldn't do anything dishonest.

SIMON: What did I tell you? If you had found the cup, we would have happily turned over the culprit. You could have killed him in any way you liked.

EGYPTIAN: Sir! We have found the cup in this sack.

JUDAH: In Benjamin's sack?

SIMON: Killed? Did I say killed? Death is so severe — and so messy!

REUVEN: Oh, no! Not Benjamin!

NARRATOR: And the brothers returned to Joseph's house, and they fell on their knees before him.

JOSEPH: Benjamin will remain with me as my servant and slave. The rest of you are free to return to your father in Canaan.

JUDAH: Master, we are all guilty. We'll all be slaves. If only we could prove our innocence.

JOSEPH: Very nice. Very sweet. However, Benjamin stays and you go. Good-bye, *shalom, bon jour, sayonara*.

Vayigash

וַיִּגַּשׁ

CAST
NARRATOR
JUDAH
BENJAMIN
JOSEPH
REUVEN
SIMON
LEVI
NAPHTALI
ISSACHAR
ASHER
GAD
ZEBULUN
JACOB
GOD
PHAROAH

NARRATOR: If ever there was a cliffhanger, this is it! When we last left our story, Joseph had decided to test his brothers' loyalty. Joseph had aged and was not recognized by his brothers. He slipped a silver cup into brother Benjamin's sack of grain, and then he accused Benjamin of stealing it. Joseph insisted that Benjamin remain with him as a slave . . . when suddenly Judah speaks up.

JUDAH: *(As fast as possible with very few breaths.)* Please, mercy, mercy! Don't you have a brother, father, mother, someone that you love? We have a father, he's old, wrinkled, worn out. And Benjamin here was born when father was already old. Benjamin's brother is dead and his mother is dead. You told us to bring him to you, but Dad refused. He was afraid to lose the little fella, but then we got so hungry that Dad had to agree. "Take my beloved son, but take care of him because his brother is dead and so is his mother, and I'll die too if he is hurt," he said. I told Dad that I'd take care of

Benjamin. If we go home without him, my father will die of grief and I will feel guilty all of my life. You don't want that old man to die. He's a sweet man. You'd like him. Take me instead. I'll stay here. Just don't take poor little Benjamin!

BENJAMIN: Look, Judah. You made the man cry. You were very good.

JOSEPH: Clear the room!

REUVEN: I guess it didn't work. Let's go.

JOSEPH: No, not you. I want all the Egyptians to leave. You Canaanites stay.

SIMON: Hey, he said that in Hebrew! I thought he was one of those foreigners.

JOSEPH: I am Joseph. Does my father still live?

JUDAH: What?

BENJAMIN: Excuse me?

SIMON: Impossible!

LEVI: Nah.

NAPHTALI: We're dreaming.

ISSACHAR: No way!

JOSEPH: Come, look at me.

ASHER: Unbelievable!

GAD: He's kidding.

ZEBULUN: Joseph is dead.

JOSEPH: That's news to me. I am Joseph, whom you sold into slavery.

REUVEN: Uh-oh.

SIMON: We're in trouble.

ASHER: I'm beginning to believe him, and we are in *big* trouble.

GAD: Joseph, it really is you!

LEVI: I'm not so sure. This could be a joke.

JOSEPH: Look closely.

ZEBULUN: Oh boy oh boy oh boy oh boy oh boy!

LEVI: Joseph, what's that old expression — forgive and forget?

JOSEPH: I'll never forget.

JUDAH: (*To Levi.*) I wish you hadn't said that.

JOSEPH: Relax, brothers.

SIMON: Relax? Relax? We throw our own brother in a pit, plan to kill him, and then sell him as a slave. Later, we tear his coat of many colors.

JOSEPH: You tore my coat of many colors?

SIMON: And we tell our father he's dead. Meanwhile, our long lost brother, whom we think is dead, now stands in front of us as Egypt's second in command. Would you relax? Would you be cheerful? Quite frankly, I'm scared to death!

JOSEPH: Don't be angry with yourselves. For after all, it was God's plan to send me here to preserve our lives.

NAPHTALI: You're not sore?

JOSEPH: Nope.

NAPHTALI: Not even a little?

JOSEPH: No.

NAPHTALI: Not even a fraction?

JUDAH: Don't push it, Naphtali.

NARRATOR: And Joseph fell upon his brother Benjamin's neck and cried, and Benjamin wept upon his neck. And he kissed all his brothers and wept, and after that his brothers talked with him.

JOSEPH: Pharaoh is pleased that you are here. He says that the whole family can come down to Egypt. The famine still has another five years to go, so return to Canaan, pack up, and bring father and the family back with you.

NARRATOR: Joseph gave them wagons and provisions in accordance with the commandment of Pharaoh. To all, he gave one change of clothes, but to Benjamin he gave five changes of clothes and 300 shekels.

JOSEPH: Don't spend it all in one place, Benjamin. Listen everyone, drive carefully. Stay on the right side of the road, and try your best to avoid robbers. Hurry back!

* * *

JACOB: My sons, you're all home.

JUDAH: Father, guess what?

REUVEN: Judah, try to be subtle. He's an old man.

SIMON: Ease into the story slowly.

JUDAH: Don't you have any faith in my common sense?

JACOB: What? What are you talking about?

JUDAH: Joseph is alive in Egypt and he is prime minister!

SIMON: Bravo, Judah. That was very subtle.

JACOB: Huh? What? Joseph?

REUVEN: That's right. He's alive!

JACOB: I don't believe it.

NAPHTALI: Look at all the things he gave us and how he spoiled Benjamin. The little guy is loaded with cash and clothes!

JACOB: It must be my son! Pack the camels. We're going to Egypt.

* * *

NARRATOR: Meanwhile, that night . . .

GOD: Jacob, Jacob.

JACOB: I am here, God. Where have You been?

GOD: Trust me, Jacob. I've been here all the time. And I tell you now, don't worry about taking everyone down into Egypt. I promise that someday I'll bring them up again.

* * *

NARRATOR: Jacob arose from Beersheva, and took his sons and households and cattle and goods, and brought them to Egypt. They were 70 in number. Joseph went in a chariot to meet his father.

JOSEPH: My father!

JACOB: Joseph, my son, my son! Now that I have seen your face, I can die in peace.

JOSEPH: Whoa, not so fast. I'd like to talk to you for awhile. And I want you to meet Pharaoh.

* * *

JOSEPH: This is my father, Jacob.

PHARAOH: So this is your family. I will give them grazing land in Goshen.

JACOB: Bless you, mighty Pharaoh.

PHARAOH: Thank you. Let me look at you. How old are you?

JACOB: Only 130.

PHARAOH: I don't know what they put in your food, but order me two tons of it.

NARRATOR: And Joseph supported his family. Joseph governed Egypt during the famine, and enlarged Pharaoh's powers and lands. The Hebrews lived in Goshen and multiplied and multiplied and multiplied.

Vayechi

ויחי

GENESIS 47:28-50:26

CAST
NARRATOR
JACOB
JOSEPH
REUVEN
SIMON
LEVI
JUDAH
ISSACHAR
DAN
ASHER
BENJAMIN
GAD

NARRATOR: And Jacob lived in Egypt for seventeen years. And he called to Joseph, his son.

JACOB: Joseph, I am 147 years old and I am getting ready to die.

JOSEPH: Father, you're still young. Your father, Isaac, lived to be 180. Abraham was 175.

JACOB: Joseph, be realistic. I want to be buried with my fathers in the Cave of Machpelah in Hebron. Promise me that this will happen.

JOSEPH: I promise, but I still think that it is too soon to think about such things. You are a very young 147-year-old, Father!

* * *

NARRATOR: And it came to pass that a short time later, Joseph was told that his father Jacob was sick.

JOSEPH: Father, I have brought you my sons Manasseh and Ephraim to be blessed.

JACOB: I've lived a full life. God appeared to me and told me that I would be fruitful and multiply. God was right.

JOSEPH: Twelve sons, a daughter, and hundreds of grandchildren. I'd say God made good on that promise, and then some.

JACOB: Joseph, your sons will be as sons to me, just as Reuven and Simon are my sons. They will both receive an inheritance just as the others. In this way, you receive an extra portion. Now bring forth your sons. I am dim of eyes.

JOSEPH: Dim of eyes?

JACOB: I'm nearly blind as was my father. I guess bad eyes run in the family.

JOSEPH: I am putting Manasseh under your right hand because he is the oldest. Ephraim is under your left hand.

JACOB: The God before whom Abraham and Isaac did walk, the God who has always been my Shepherd, the angel who redeemed me from evil, bless these lads.

JOSEPH: Father, I hesitate to interrupt, but you've switched hands. You are blessing Ephraim as the firstborn.

JACOB: Joseph, I know what I'm doing.

JOSEPH: But you're blessing the wrong child!

JACOB: Manasseh will be a great people, but this younger brother will be even greater.

JOSEPH: How do you know that?

JACOB: Joseph, do you think you're the only person with the gift of seeing the future? Now call your brothers so that I may bless each of them.

REUVEN: I wonder what Jacob is going to say?

SIMON: I'm worried. I have never been exactly obedient.

LEVI: I guess this is where everybody gets what he deserves.

JACOB: Reuven, my firstborn, you pulled a few fast ones on me. You shall be as unstable as water.

REUVEN: I should have stayed home.

JACOB: Simon and Levi

LEVI: We can come back later, if you'd like.

JACOB: You are both violent men. You killed in anger. I curse your anger, for it is fierce and cruel. I will scatter you among the other tribes.

SIMON: Was that a blessing?

LEVI: Considering the way we have acted, let's think of it as a blessing.

JACOB: Judah, you are a lion's cub.

JUDAH: I am?

JACOB: Your brothers will bow to you, and the staff of leadership will not depart from your hand.

JUDAH: Whew, I passed!

JACOB: Issachar.

JUDAH: He's hiding behind the furniture.

JACOB: Issachar, you are like a large-boned donkey. You bend down among sheep. Where you see a nice resting place, you will sit, even if it means being a servant to others.

ISSACHAR: That's better than being like unstable water. I'll take it.

JACOB: You have no choice. Zebulun, you shall dwell by the shore and build ships. Dan, you will be like a serpent in the road that bites the horse's heels so that the rider falls backwards.

DAN: What does that mean?

JACOB: I haven't time to explain. Read the Book of Judges. Gad, you'll be like an army that first is beaten and then fights back. Asher, your foot shall be in oil, your bread shall be fat, and you shall yield much royal food.

ASHER: It sounds messy . . . but good!

JACOB: Naphtali shall give out goodly words. Joseph will be a fruitful vine by a water fountain. He has been scorned, but stood firm. He will truly be blessed. The blessings of your father shall be on your head like a crown. Benjamin, you will be like a wolf that in the morning eats his prey and in the evening divides the spoil.

BENJAMIN: Father, I thought I was one of your favorites. What does that mean?

JACOB: Sorry, son. I call 'em like I see 'em. That concludes the blessings. When I die, I am to be buried with my fathers and mothers in the Cave of Machpelah in Canaan, which

Abraham bought from Ephron the Hittite. There Abraham and Sarah are buried. There, too, my father Isaac and mother Rebekah are buried. There is where I buried your mother Leah.

REUVEN: Father, don't die!

JOSEPH: He is no more.

NARRATOR: Jacob died and Joseph fell on his face, wept upon him, and kissed him. The Egyptians embalmed Jacob and mourned for seventy days. Pharaoh gave Joseph permission to go to Canaan to bury Jacob. And the sons carried Jacob to Canaan, and buried him in the Cave of Machpelah.

* * *

LEVI: Joseph, now that Jacob is dead, are you going to harm us?

GAD: Remember that Dad said to forgive our sins.

JOSEPH: I told you once already that all will be okay. You meant evil against me, but God meant it for good. Now, let's return to our good life in Egypt.

NARRATOR: Joseph lived 110 years. He lived to see his great-grandchildren. And he said to his brothers . . .

JOSEPH: I can't believe you tore up my colored coat!

NARRATOR: And also . . .

JOSEPH: When God takes you out of Egypt to the land that was promised to Abraham, Isaac, and Jacob, swear that you will carry my bones with you.

NARRATOR: When Joseph died, they embalmed him and placed him in a coffin in Egypt.

ALL: This concludes the Book of Genesis. *Chazak, chazak, v'nitchazayk* — be strong, be strong, and let us be strengthened.

Shemot

CAST
NARRATOR
ANNOUNCER
HEBREW 1
HEBREW 2
PHARAOH
MINISTER
SLAVE
PRINCESS
MOSES
GOD
AARON

NARRATOR: This is the first *parashah* (or section) of the Book of Exodus, entitled *Shemot*, which means names. It begins: These are the names of the sons of Israel who came to Egypt with Jacob: Reuven, Simon, Levi, Judah, Issachar, Zebulun, Benjamin, Dan, Naphtali, Gad, and Asher. The total number was seventy. Joseph was already in Egypt. And the children of Israel multiplied, and the land was full of them.

ANNOUNCER: Extra, extra! Read all about it! New king in Egypt!

HEBREW 1: I hope the new Pharaoh treats us as nicely as the other kings. I hope he remembers the things that Joseph did for Egypt many, many years ago.

ANNOUNCER: Extra, extra! Read all about it! Pharaoh decides to make the Hebrews slaves! Pharaoh forces slaves to build cities!

HEBREW 2: What got under his collar? What did we ever do to him? We're minding our own business, not bothering anybody, and boom! Just like that, he has us building the store cities of Pitom and Ramses.

HEBREW 1: At least we don't have to build pyramids. Aren't they the most ridiculous looking things you've ever seen?

* * *

PHARAOH: Minister, come here!

MINISTER: Yes, great Pharaoh, ruler of Egypt, son of the sun god, master of the Nile . . .

PHARAOH: All right, all right, enough already. What's the story with the Hebrew slaves?

MINISTER: They're still around.

PHARAOH: I know that. They're everywhere! They multiply like rabbits. The more work I give them, the more babies they have. We've got to get rid of them! Do you have any ideas?

MINISTER: Why don't you let them go?

PHARAOH: That's a pretty stupid idea.

MINISTER: Maybe, if you asked them nicely, they'd stop having so many babies.

PHARAOH: You want me to ask them nicely to stop having babies? I'm the Pharaoh, ruler of Egypt, son of the sun god, master of the Nile! I don't ask anyone anything nicely. In fact, I don't ask — I act. I'd rather just kill them all.

MINISTER: But who would finish the store cities?

PHARAOH: Drat, you're right. We'll have to do it slowly. We'll kill all the babies.

MINISTER: That could be awfully messy.

PHARAOH: All right, just the male babies. Kill them as they are born. Have the boy babies thrown into the Nile.

MINISTER: But they'll drown.

PHARAOH: Bingo!

* * *

NARRATOR: A certain man of the house of Levi went and married a Levite woman. She bore a son, and when she saw how beautiful he was, she hid him for three months. When she could care for him no longer, she put the child into a basket and placed it among the reeds of the Nile River.

SLAVE: Look, Princess. There's a basket floating in the water.

PRINCESS: Pull it in and let's see what's inside. Oooh, a baby! Kitchy, kitchy koo. Where did he come from?

SLAVE: Probably from a mommy and daddy.

PRINCESS: Most likely a Hebrew child. But I think I'll keep him. What shall I name him?

SLAVE: How about Basket, since that is what he's floating in?

PRINCESS: Basket is a funny name.

SLAVE: What about Irving? You can call him Irving.

PRINCESS: No, he shall be called Moses, for I drew him out of the water.

SLAVE: I like Irving better.

* * *

NARRATOR: Some time later, Moses grew up and he went out to see the suffering of his Hebrew brothers and sisters. He saw an Egyptian beating a Hebrew. He looked around to see if anyone was watching, then he struck down the Egyptian and hid him in the sand. The next day, Moses saw two Hebrews fighting.

MOSES: Hey, there. Stop that!

HEBREW 1: *(Mimicking.)* Hey, there. Stop that. Who made you king, Mr. Big Shot, Mr. Fancy Shmancy Egyptian prince? Are you going to kill me like you killed that Egyptian yesterday?

MOSES: That's supposed to be a secret!

HEBREW 2: Secret? It's all over the country. Your name is already on the most wanted tablets

MOSES: I've got to escape!

* * *

NARRATOR: Moses fled to the land of Midian, and stayed with Jethro and his seven daughters. He married Jethro's daughter Zipporah, and had two sons named Gershom and Eliezer.

GOD: There is a lot of moaning going on down there in Egypt. It is time to remember My covenant with Abraham — my promise that his family would inherit Canaan. The old Pharaoh is dead and there is a new one. Yes, it is time.

NARRATOR: Moses was tending the sheep of his father-in-law Jethro, and he drove the flock toward Mount Horeb, the mountain of God.

MOSES: Look at that! A burning bush — it's on fire, but it's not burning up. That is incredible! How is it doing that? I've got to move in closer for a better look.

GOD: Moses! Moses!

MOSES: Here I am. Who said that? Where are you?

GOD: Don't come any closer. Remove your sandals, for you are standing on holy ground.

MOSES: Who is talking?

GOD: I am the God of your fathers — Abraham, Isaac, and Jacob.

MOSES: Oh! Sorry to disturb You. I'll just leave quietly. Nice bush, by the way.

GOD: Stay, Moses. It's time to rescue the Hebrew people from slavery, and bring them into a land flowing with milk and honey.

MOSES: That's a very nice idea.

GOD: I shall send you to Pharaoh and you shall free the Hebrews.

MOSES: Me? You must have made a mistake — I'm a wanted criminal.

GOD: You, Moses.

MOSES: All right, suppose I go? When the Hebrews ask, who shall I say sent me?

GOD: I Am that I Am. The Being of the universe sends you. You tell them that.

MOSES: What about Pharaoh? What if he doesn't listen to me?

GOD: He will listen. Throw your rod down.

MOSES: This rod is important to me. I tend sheep and climb hills with it. Oh, okay, I'll throw it down. Hey, it's turned into a snake!

GOD: Pick it up.

MOSES: Pick up a snake?

GOD: Trust me, Moses.

MOSES: Okay. Ho! It turned back into a rod. Excellent!

GOD: Good. Now go.

MOSES: But I can't speak to Pharaoh. I stu, stu, stu, stutter.

GOD: If necessary, your brother Aaron can act as spokesperson. Even now, he's coming to greet you. Now move along.

* * *

NARRATOR: Moses and Aaron gathered the elders of Israel, and repeated the words which God had spoken to Moses, and they performed the signs, and the people were convinced. Afterward, Moses and Aaron went to Pharaoh.

MOSES: Pharaoh, hello. I'm Moses and this is Aaron. We have a favor to ask you.

PHARAOH: Go right ahead. What can I do for you?

MOSES: Thus says the God of Israel — Let my people go that they may worship Me.

PHARAOH: Sure! Why not? What a small thing to ask of me. What do I need 600,000 slaves for anyway? All they're good for is building storage cities and monuments.

MOSES: Aaron, that was easy.

AARON: Moses, I don't think the Pharaoh is serious.

PHARAOH: You're right, I'm not serious! Who is your God? I don't see any God around here. Get out!

MOSES: We'll only be gone three days.

PHARAOH: Three days? That's reasonable.

AARON: Moses, I think you're convincing him.

MOSES: Aaron, I don't think this Pharaoh is the generous type.

PHARAOH: Moses, to show you how impressed I am, I'm going to make your Hebrews collect their own straw to make bricks. And I'll beat any slave that doesn't meet the quota.

MOSES: How can you do such a cruel thing?

PHARAOH: How? I just did it!

NARRATOR: And the Hebrews came to Moses and Aaron and they said to them: May God punish you for what you have done to us!

MOSES: We sure are in a mess. Instead of freeing the slaves, we've made things worse.

GOD: Moses, don't worry. It's only temporary. Everything's going according to plan. Pharaoh will let you go. He will soon know a power greater than his own.

Vaera

וארא

EXODUS 6:2-9:35

CAST
NARRATOR
HEBREWS
MOSES
GOD
PHARAOH
AARON
MINISTER
EGYPTIAN 1
EGYPTIAN 2
EGYPTIAN 3

NARRATOR: When we last left our story, the Hebrew slaves were in a perilous situation.

HEBREWS: Woe to us! We are in a perilous situation!

NARRATOR: A new Pharaoh had arisen in the land who made slaves of the Hebrews. Moses was sent by God to free the people, but Pharaoh refused to listen to Moses. Instead, he increased the bitterness of slavery. When we last saw Moses, he was depressed and demoralized.

MOSES: I am depressed and demoralized.

GOD: Moses, I am the Almighty who appeared to Abraham, Isaac, and Jacob as *El Shaddai*. I have heard the suffering of the Hebrews and remembered My covenant with them.

MOSES: But nobody will listen to me. The Hebrews won't pay attention, Pharaoh is cruel and mean, and I stu, stu, stutter.

GOD: Do not lose heart, Moses. I am placing you in the role of God to Pharaoh, and your brother Aaron is as your prophet. Now go, show Pharaoh the power I have given you.

* * *

NARRATOR: Moses was eighty years old and Aaron eighty-three when they made their demand on Pharaoh.

PHARAOH: Look who's back — Moses and Aaron. And you brought a rod with you! A game? Baseball, high jump, pool?

MOSES: Aaron, throw the rod down.

AARON: Okay, bro.

PHARAOH: A snake — how impressive! My magicians can do that, too.

MOSES: Aaron, their rods have all turned into snakes also.

AARON: I'll try a harder trick.

MINISTER: Pharaoh, Aaron's snake has swallowed the snakes of all our magicians!

PHARAOH: Big deal.

MOSES: God, Pharaoh was not impressed by the snake trick

GOD: He is a stubborn man.

MOSES: What do we do?

GOD: Do as I say. It's time Egypt had a few plagues. In the morning, go to Pharaoh by the edge of the Nile and strike the water with your rod. The river shall turn into blood and all the fish will die.

* * *

MINISTER: Good morning, great Pharaoh. Would you like a cup of water?

PHARAOH: Yes, thank you. Look, over there! Do you see them? It's Aaron and Moses. What are those pests up to now?

MINISTER: I haven't the foggiest idea. Here's your glass of blood.

PHARAOH: Blood?!

MINISTER: Blood!!! The water just turned to blood! The whole Nile is turning red! It must be the work of Moses.

MOSES: Let my people go, Pharaoh, or the land will become infested with frogs.

NARRATOR: And Aaron held out his arm over the rivers, the canals, and the ponds, and frogs came up and covered the land.

MINISTER: Pharaoh, what are we going to do? If I step on one more frog, I'll scream. Last night, I shared my bed with forty-nine frogs. My baby's first words were goo, goo, ribbet.

PHARAOH: Moses, ask God to remove these frogs and I'll let your people go.

NARRATOR: But once the frogs were gone, Pharaoh became stubborn again.

MINISTER: Pharaoh, there are some Egyptian peasants here to see you.

EGYPTIAN 1: Mighty Pharaoh.

EGYPTIAN 2: Master of the Nile.

EGYPTIAN 3: Son of the sun god.

PHARAOH: Get down to business.

EGYPTIAN 1: We can take a joke as well as the next nation, but enough is enough!

EGYPTIAN 2: First we have to drink blood water. Then we share our beds with frogs. When you promised to let the Hebrews go, things cleared up for a while.

EGYPTIAN 3: Then you got stubborn, so we get lice. Everybody but the Hebrews are scratching like crazy! Next we get swarms of insects.

EGYPTIAN 1: You know, it's very hard to do business when there are swarms of insects. Then comes pestilence. All of our farm animals are lying sick. But does Pharaoh let the Hebrews go? Noooooo . . . he's hard-hearted.

EGYPTIAN 2: Last week, everyone breaks out in boils. The dermatologists had patients lined up for blocks! This week, it's hailing. Each hailstone is the size of a cow's hoof!

EGYPTIAN 3: Pharaoh, we're patient people, but have mercy on us! These plagues are making us neurotic. What do you say, mighty Pharaoh?

PHARAOH: Off with your heads!

EGYPTIAN 3: Is that your final answer?

NARRATOR: So Pharaoh remained stubborn and he would not let the Hebrews go . . . just as God had foretold through Moses.

Bo   בא

CAST
NARRATOR
MOSES
MINISTER
PHARAOH
AARON
GOD

NARRATOR: Our top story tonight: After weeks of blood water, frogs, swarming insects, pestilence, boils, and hail, Pharaoh has consented to meet once more with Moses and Aaron, leaders of the "Let My People Go" committee.

MOSES: Pharaoh, let my people go! How long will you be hard-hearted?

MINISTER: Pharaoh, perhaps you should listen to Moses.

PHARAOH: Nobody threatens the great Pharaoh!

MOSES: If you refuse to let my people go, says the God of the Hebrews, I will bring locusts to your territory. What the hail didn't destroy, the locusts will eat. They'll eat everything from grain stalks to chin whiskers.

PHARAOH: You can't threaten me.

MINISTER: Oh great Pharaoh, we really didn't want locusts. There is no market for locusts. Lighten up, oh wondrous leader.

PHARAOH: Be gone from here, Hebrew nobodies!

MOSES: Nobodies? My, my, my. We certainly are getting touchy.

* * *

NARRATOR: And locusts invaded the land of Egypt in a thick mass. They hid the land from view, for the land was covered with them. They ate all the grasses of the fields and the fruits of the trees so that nothing green remained in Egypt. And Pharaoh summoned Moses and Aaron.

PHARAOH: Friends, dear friends, buddies, pals!

AARON: And now I suppose we should think he's serious? I don't trust him.

PHARAOH: Hey, I've sinned! I made a mistake. I stand guilty. Can you forgive me?

MOSES: Will you let us go?

PHARAOH: Friend, buddy, pal! You scratch my back, I'll scratch yours, so to speak.

MOSES: Very well. With a strong west wind God will lift the locusts from the land. Now, about your part of the bargain . . .

PHARAOH: Bargain? Hah! You're lucky to be alive. Scram, get out of here!

AARON: I guess this means that you still won't let us go.

PHARAOH: Hey, who turned out the lights? Where did everyone go?

MINISTER: We seem to be having a blackout, Pharaoh.

PHARAOH: Ouch, you're standing on my foot! It's the middle of the day and I can't see one *argmah* in front of my face!

MINISTER: Moses just pointed his staff toward the sky, and suddenly there is this giant cloud of darkness.

PHARAOH: Moses again. Ow, you're sitting on my hand! That's it. Call Moses!

MOSES: You rang?

PHARAOH: Get rid of the darkness and I'll let the slaves go.

MOSES: This is the last time, Pharaoh. We and our cattle and our families and our possessions must be allowed to leave.

PHARAOH: Okay, okay!

MOSES: There. The darkness is gone.

PHARAOH: Ah, there you are. Listen you, I will decide when and if you go. If I ever see you again, I shall kill you.

MOSES: Pharaoh, you're right. You shall not see me again. But your people shall come begging that we be allowed to leave.

GOD: Moses, this is the Almighty.

MOSES: Yes, God, I am here. What do we do next? The darkness was very effective. Pharaoh is going nuts. But he is one hard-hearted fellow. Nine plagues haven't softened him up at all.

GOD: It is time for the final plague, Moses. Are you ready?

MOSES: Final? As in death?

GOD: Tell all your people to ask for jewelry and gold and silver and clothing from their Egyptian neighbors. Toward midnight, every firstborn in the land of Egypt shall die.

AARON: But we live in Egypt. Are we going to die, too?

GOD: Good question. This month shall be the first month of the year. We might as well start a calendar if you're going to be your own nation. On the tenth of the month, take a lamb, and on the fourteenth, you shall sacrifice it and eat it roasted. Then take of its blood and mark the doorposts of your houses. Those homes with blood markings, I shall pass over.

AARON: Pass over? What a great name for this night! Passover.

MOSES: It's certainly better than Bloody Door Day.

GOD: This day shall be remembered always. Seven days you shall celebrate this event. No one shall eat leavened bread from the fourteenth to the twenty-first of this month. Now, I hope you remember everything I said. Go tell the people.

NARRATOR: In the middle of the night, God struck down all the firstborn in the land of Egypt, from the firstborn of Pharaoh to the firstborn of the captive in the dungeon, and all the firstborn of the cattle. Pharaoh summoned Aaron and Moses in the middle of the night.

PHARAOH: Get out of here! Go! Leave us alone. Take our gold and silver. Leave now. *Adios. Au revoir. Sayonara.* Go! And before you go, bless me.

AARON: Why, Moses — I do think that Pharaoh is letting our people go!

MOSES: Now I think he's serious!

NARRATOR: In haste, the Hebrews left on foot. About 600,000, plus the children. And they baked unleavened bread in haste. The length of time that they lived in Egypt was 430 years. And God commanded Moses and Aaron: For seven days there shall be no leavened bread eaten. Since God saved the firstborn, let all firstborn animals be sacrificed to God, and let all firstborn male children be redeemed. By strength of hand the Almighty brought us out of Egypt, out of the house of bondage.

Beshalach

בשלח

EXODUS 13:17-17:16

CAST
NARRATOR
PHARAOH
MINISTER 1
MINISTER 2
ISRAELITE 1
ISRAELITE 2
MOSES
ISRAELITE 3
GOD
AARON

NARRATOR: God led the Children of Israel by the way of the Sea of Reeds, And Moses took the bones of Joseph with him to bury in the Cave of Machpelah. And a pillar of cloud led them by day, and a pillar of fire led them by night. Meanwhile, back in Egypt . . .

PHARAOH: Ministers, why isn't my breakfast ready?

MINISTER 1: Mighty Pharaoh, we are interviewing cooks today. It's been hard to find replacements.

MINISTER 2: Speaking of which, we've got some store cities that have to be finished. We need new workers.

MINISTER 1: Remember the good old days when there were Hebrew slaves?

PHARAOH: When there were frogs and lice and lots of plagues?

MINISTER 2: When Pharaoh could count on having breakfast in bed.

MINISTER 1: When all the firstborn were dead?

PHARAOH: Blast them! We were fools to let them go. Saddle the horses! Get the chariots warmed up! Let's bring them back!

* * *

ISRAELITE 1: This is the life. Free at last, free at last. God gives us a pillar of cloud by day and a pillar of fire by night to lead us. What a nice life!

ISRAELITE 2: Woe, woe, woe!

ISRAELITE 1: God will protect us all the way to Canaan.

ISRAELITE 2: Oh, oh, oh!

ISRAELITE 1: What is the problem? Relax, God will protect us.

ISRAELITE 2: Guess again. Look behind us — I think I see Pharaoh and the Egyptians coming!

ISRAELITE 1: Help! Help! We're going to die!

ISRAELITE 2: Won't God protect us?

ISRAELITE 1: There are 600 chariots breathing down our necks. Be practical — scream. Help! Help!

MOSES: Everyone remain calm!

ISRAELITE 1: Easy for you to say, Moses. It looks like we have a choice: We can drown in the sea, or go back to Egypt. Let's hear it for slavery!

MOSES: There is a choice. Everyone, start walking into the water . . . now!

ISRAELITE 2: You're crazy. We'll drown!

NARRATOR: And Moses held out his arm over the sea, and the Almighty drove back the sea and turned it into dry land. And the pillar of cloud came between the army of Egypt and the Israelites.

ISRAELITE 1: Like I told you all along, God will protect us.

MINISTER 1: Do you see that, Pharaoh? The sea has parted! Let's go home. I'll make breakfast for you myself.

PHARAOH: The Israelites are on the other side. If they can cross the sea, we can, too. Order the chariots into the sea!

ISRAELITE 2: Moses is spreading his arm out over the sea and the waters are returning to normal. The Egyptians are drowning!

ISRAELITE 1: Yes, it's the old drown in the sea trick. Works every time.

NARRATOR: Moses and the Children of Israel sang songs of praise — *"Mee Chamocha BaAyleem Adonai; Mee Kamocha Ne'edar BaKodesh?"* And Miriam led the women in dance and song.

* * *

MOSES: All right, we'll stop here at Marah for the night.

ISRAELITE 3: Woe that we have left Egypt! The water of Marah smells funny.

MOSES: I shall make it sweet for you. Now stop complaining. Next stop is Elim, where there are 70 palm trees and 12 wells of water.

ISRAELITE 1: Woe to us that we left Egypt! We are hungry. At least in Egypt we always had bread to eat and a good stew now and then.

MOSES: One more "Woe to us" and I'll scream! My goodness, you're a picky people. First you want water, and now you want food.

GOD: Moses, go easy on them. If they want bread, I'll give them bread. We'll call it manna. The people will gather it every morning Sunday through Friday. Since we don't work on Shabbat, they will gather a double load on Friday.

ISRAELITE 2: What is this strange frost all over the place? It feels doughy, like bread.

ISRAELITE 1: Hey, everybody, this stuff is good! I got rye.

ISRAELITE 2: Mine's whole wheat.

NARRATOR: And the Israelites ate manna for forty years until they came to a settled land. From the Wilderness of Zin, they traveled to Rephidim.

ISRAELITE 3: Woe to us! There is no water here. We'll all die!

MOSES: God, what do I do? These people are driving me crazy!

GOD: Moses, calm down. They're still a little edgy. Take your rod and strike the rock. Water will come forth.

MOSES: Okay, but sooner or later these people are going to have to stop complaining. I'm getting severe headaches.

NARRATOR: And Moses brought forth water from the rock. And they called the place Massah and Meriba, for they tried the Almighty to know if God would help them.

* * *

AARON: Moses, come quick! We've got problems.

MOSES: What's the matter now?

AARON: We're being attacked by the evil nation of Amalek.

MOSES: Joshua, choose an army of good fighters and go meet Amalek. I will go to the top of a hill with my rod.

NARRATOR: Moses stood on the top of the hill with the rod in his hand. Whenever he held his hand up, the Israelites would start winning, but when his hand dropped, the Amalekites prevailed.

AARON: Moses, keep your hands up.

MOSES: I can't. They are like lead. You try keeping your hands in the air for an hour!

NARRATOR: So Aaron and a man named Hur stood on either side of Moses and supported his hands. And Joshua defeated Amalek that day. Cursed be Amalek. Let his name be blotted out!

Yitro

יתרו

EXODUS 18:1-20:23

CAST
JETHRO
SECRETARY
MOSES
NARRATOR
GOD
ISRAELITE 1
ISRAELITE 2
ISRAELITE 3

JETHRO: Excuse me, I'd like to see Moses.

SECRETARY: Do you have an appointment?

JETHRO: No.

SECRETARY: I can make one for you, but I doubt you could get in to see him before next Tuesday.

JETHRO: But I've traveled a long way to see him.

SECRETARY: We've all traveled a long way. Egypt isn't exactly down the street and around the corner, you know.

JETHRO: No, no. I'm from Midian. I am Jethro, Moses' father-in-law. And I have come with my daughter — his wife, Zipporah, and his sons Gershom and Eliezer.

SECRETARY: It's a nice family you have there.

JETHRO: So, can we see Moses now?

SECRETARY: Like I said, next Tuesday. Yesterday, Moses' "cousins" were here. And this lady claims to be his niece twice

102

removed. Everyone in this line claims to be related to Moses, but it won't get you into the tent any sooner.

JETHRO: But I really am his father-in-law!

SECRETARY: And I'm the Pharaoh of Egypt, and that guy over there is the king of the Philistines.

MOSES: Excuse me, no more appointments for today. I am getting tired. From dawn to dusk all week long! My strength is gone.

JETHRO: Moses!

MOSES: Jethro! Zipporah!

SECRETARY: Jethro! Sir! You can take a little joke. I knew it was you. Just a little mistake. I'll go water your camel and apply for unemployment.

NARRATOR: Moses told his father-in-law everything that God had done to Pharaoh and to the Egyptians.

JETHRO: Truly the Almighty is greater than all gods. I shall offer sacrifices unto God.

NARRATOR: The next day, Moses sat as a judge while the people stood about Moses again from morning to evening.

JETHRO: Moses, what are you doing?

MOSES: I'm judging the people. I have to make the laws of God known to the people.

JETHRO: It seems like a tough job. One judge for 600,000 people.

MOSES: If I work all day every day for the next five weeks, I'll be pretty much caught up.

JETHRO: Either that or you'll be dead. Why don't you find some honest people, whom you trust, to help judge the people?

MOSES: Because . . .

JETHRO: Because why?

MOSES: Because I never thought of that!

NARRATOR: So Moses appointed judges over the people, and they judged the people at all times, and the difficult matters they brought to Moses.

* * *

GOD: Moses, climb up this mountain and we'll talk. I think we're ready for Phase Two

MOSES: Phase Two? I'm still recovering from Phase One.

GOD: Go remind the people that I took them out of Egypt on eagles' wings. They shall be my people — a kingdom of Priests and a holy people. And I shall be their God. Three days from now, I shall appear in a thick cloud that all may hear Me. Therefore, prepare the people.

MOSES: How do I prepare the people for such an occasion?

GOD: Have them wash their clothes. Everyone should be clean and look like a *mensch**. Also, I want people to act pure. When the ram's horn is sounded, the people are to gather at the bottom of the mountain, but no one is to touch the mountain. Death to one who touches the mountain.

ISRAELITE 1: This is very scary. What do I wear to meet God? What do I say? Hello, how are You? How's everything upstairs?

* a person of good character

104

ISRAELITE 2: The horn is sounding! Look, the mountain is covered in smoke. What's that other sound?

ISRAELITE 3: It's my knees shaking.

ISRAELITE 1: The mountain is trembling and God is talking with thunder!

ISRAELITE 2: And over there are fire and clouds! That horn is deafening.

MOSES: Wait here while I go up the mountain to speak with God.

ISRAELITE 2: Good, you go, we'll stay here and shake in fear.

* * *

MOSES: God, I think you're scaring the people.

GOD: Fear is one means of getting their attention. Thunder and fire are very effective.

MOSES: Very effective! You're scaring me, too.

GOD: Go down and tell the people these words: These are the first laws, the Ten Commandments. I am your God. You shall have no other gods before Me. You shall make no graven images. Do not take My name in vain. Remember the Sabbath to keep it holy. Honor your father and mother. Don't murder. Don't commit adultery. Don't steal. Don't bear false witness. Don't covet your neighbor's possessions.

* * *

ISRAELITE 2: Moses, why don't you speak for us to God? We're scared to death!

MOSES: Come closer everyone.

ISRAELITE 3: You mean, get closer to a mountain that is covered in clouds, spitting fire, hurling thunder and lightning, and smoking all at the same time?

MOSES: Remember the words which you have heard this day. Make no gods for yourselves. I shall return to the mountain. Stay here. I'll fill you in later. I'll take good notes.

Mishpatim מִשְׁפָּטִים

CAST
ANNOUNCER
AARON
DEBBIE
KORACH
ELIEZER

ANNOUNCER: Ladies and gentlemen, it's time for everyone's very favorite game show — number one in the Bible ratings for forty years — "Let's Play *Mishpatim*!" Now, the rules of the game are simple. We give contestants a situation, and they guess the solution according to the biblical section called *Mishpatim*. Aaron, High Priest, who do we have to play the game tonight?

AARON: First of all, Eliezer Ben Simon . . . come on down! Korach Ben Abihu . . . come on down! And finally, Debbie Goldberg . . . come on down! You are today's contestants on "Let's Play *Mishpatim*!"

ANNOUNCER: Okay, players, here's the first situation. If you acquire a Hebrew slave for six years, he goes free in the seventh. What happens if he doesn't want his freedom?

DEBBIE: Force him to go free anyway!

ANNOUNCER: Nope. Korach?

KORACH: Kill him!

ANNOUNCER: Kind of messy. How about it, Eliezer?

ELIEZER: I don't know. There are so many laws in the chapters of *Mishpatim*. I'll take a wild guess. Why don't you staple him to the door?

ANNOUNCER: You're right!

ELIEZER: I am?

ANNOUNCER: A slave who wants to stay with his master is brought to the door, and his master shall pierce his ear with an awl. Bonus time! What happens if a man intentionally murders someone?

ELIEZER: If it happened to me, I'd murder him back.

ANNOUNCER: We'll accept that. A man who kills another intentionally shall be put to death. Eliezer, you've got 30 points. Players, here's the next question. Two men are fighting and damage occurs. Fill in the sentence. An eye for an eye, a tooth for a _____.

ELIEZER: Toothbrush?

ANNOUNCER: Wrong.

DEBBIE: Tooth. Eye for an eye, tooth for a tooth, hand for a hand.

ANNOUNCER: That's right! Bonus time for Debbie. If you start a fire and it spreads, what happens?

DEBBIE: It burns a lot of things?

ANNOUNCER: I'm sorry. Whoever started the fire must pay people whose property is damaged. But you do get 20 points. Okay, players, situation number three . . . true or false: God commands that you pick on strangers, widows, orphans, and poor people. Eliezer?

ELIEZER: God seems pretty tough. I say true.

ANNOUNCER: Nice try, Eliezer. How about you, Korach?

KORACH: I'll say false. God commands that you not treat strangers badly because we were strangers in Egypt, and tells us not to mistreat orphans or widows or poor people.

ANNOUNCER: Incredible and correct. What a player!

AARON: May we interrupt for a moment? Someone's ox got loose outside the tent and it is attacking the other oxen as well as several people. The penalty for the injury caused by this animal ranges from the animal being stoned to the owner being stoned.

ANNOUNCER: Thanks for the information. It looks like quite a bit of the studio audience is leaving the tent. Apparently, the ox got their goat. Korach, your bonus question is to fill in this blank. Don't cook a kid in its mother's _____.

KORACH: Pressure cooker?

ANNOUNCER: Sorry. The correct law reads: Don't cook a kid — a baby goat — in its mother's milk. Adding up the points as round one comes to an end, Eliezer is in the lead. Round two is fast and furious. Call out the answer as quickly as possible. Three times a year a festival is held for the Almighty when all males must appear before God. Name these three festivals.

KORACH: Passover!

ANNOUNCER: Right.

DEBBIE: Feast of the Harvest — Shavuot.

ANNOUNCER: Right.

ELIEZER: Lincoln's birthday!

ANNOUNCER: Incorrect.

DEBBIE: Feast of the Ingathering — Sukkot.

ANNOUNCER: You got it! Debbie Goldberg, you're our grand prize winner!

DEBBIE: What do I get?

ANNOUNCER: You will go to the foot of the fiery Mount Sinai with Moses and the seventy elders of Israel to offer sacrifices to God. Then you will wait at the foot of the mountain until Moses comes down from speaking with God alone. Debbie?

ELIEZER: She fainted.

Terumah תרומה

CAST
BEZALEL
PERSON 1
MOSES
PERSON 2

BEZALEL: Business is really slow these days. Ever since we left Egypt, jobs have been hard to come by. When Moses isn't around, things seem to come to a standstill. He's been on that mountain for days now.

PERSON 1: Well, I don't know whether construction is the best business to be in out here in the wilderness.

BEZALEL: Things have to get better.

PERSON 1: They can't get any worse. Who wants to build storage cities with all of this moving around? Tents! Everyone owns tents. Tents are going to be the death of the construction industry.

MOSES: Excuse me, is this the Bezalel Construction Company?

BEZALEL: Yes it is.

MOSES: I was wondering if you might be interested in some business.

PERSON 1: Well, we are sort of busy.

BEZALEL: Umm . . . right! And we don't build tents.

MOSES: This would be a big contract.

BEZALEL: It would have to be. We only deal with big clients, and we are *so* busy.

MOSES: I can see how busy you are! Don't worry. I guarantee that you couldn't get a more important client.

BEZALEL: Hey, I've dealt with Pharaoh, several tribal chiefs, and some pretty wealthy people. Who's the client?

MOSES: The Almighty God.

BEZALEL: Really? God would rank right up there among the very biggest.

MOSES: That's right. God has revealed to me the plans for a Tabernacle and Holy Ark. By the way, do you do interiors?

BEZALEL: Do we do interiors? Of course! It's our specialty.

MOSES: Good. The Holy One has also ordered furniture for the Tabernacle.

BEZALEL: A tent? Oh well, so now we're in the tent business. Why don't you tell me exactly what is needed. I'll write it down.

MOSES: Everything must be made of gold, silver, copper, linen . . .

BEZALEL: Any particular color linen?

MOSES: Blue, purple, and crimson.

BEZALEL: Beautiful! There is a feel here for color coordination.

MOSES: Also . . . ram skins dyed red, oil, precious stones, perfumes, and acacia wood.

BEZALEL: Jack, could you see if we have any acacia wood in stock?

PERSON 2: I'll get right on it.

MOSES: The Ark will be made of acacia wood with two gold *cherubim* hovering over the top.

BEZALEL: Whoa! What are *cherubim*?

MOSES: Baby angels.

BEZALEL: Precious! I love the whole concept. I bet that this *cherubim* idea catches on all over the Middle East.

MOSES: For furnishings, God wants a table made of acacia wood, a *menorah* of pure gold, and all the jars and bowls made of pure gold. The outside of the Tabernacle is to be made of goat's hair.

BEZALEL: Goat's hair? Hmm. Very natural. Modest, but elegant.

MOSES: Also, there has to be a curtain of blue, crimson, and purple yarn to separate the Holy Ark from the rest of the Tabernacle.

BEZALEL: Yes! Yes! I see it. I have just the right tailor.

MOSES: For the outer courtyard, God wants the altar made of acacia wood.

BEZALEL: Jack, hurry up with that acacia wood! That particular wood is rare, you know. Pine paneling would be cheaper.

MOSES: If the plan calls for acacia wood, are you going to argue?

BEZALEL: Argue with the One who split the sea? No way. Acacia wood you want, acacia wood you get.

MOSES: Finally, the courtyard should have hangings of twisted linen with hooks of silver and purple, blue and crimson yarn. All the vessels should be made of copper.

BEZALEL: Elegant! Gorgeous! Such taste! Impeccable!

MOSES: Just remember to use all the measurements I give you exactly. These are the instructions that God gave on Mount Sinai, and we dare not change them.

BEZALEL: No problem. Bezalel Construction Company is ready to serve. And we're bonded!

Tetzaveh   תְּצַוֶּה

EXODUS 27:20-30:10

CAST
MOSES
GOD
ANNOUNCER
CALLER 1
CALLER 2
SECRETARY

MOSES: Well, Holy One, Blessed be You, I've received the Ten Commandments and instructions for constructing the Tabernacle and the Holy Ark. Does that about wrap it up?

GOD: Moses, you've just begun to learn the laws that you will teach the Israelites.

MOSES: It's been twenty days. My fingers hurt from taking notes.

GOD: Pace yourself, Moses. We're only half done. Light!

MOSES: No thanks, I don't smoke.

GOD: No, no, no. A light. We should have a light within the Tent. An eternal light.

MOSES: A *Ner Tamid* using only pure olive oil, placed just in front of the curtain.

GOD: Let's talk about your brother Aaron. He and his sons Nadab, Abihu, Eleazar, and Ithamar shall serve Me as priests. They will need special clothes. Clothes are a sign of respect sometimes. We can't have priests dressed like camel drivers.

ANNOUNCER: Good afternoon and welcome to Bible Fashion Line. Go ahead, you're on the air.

CALLER 1: I've heard that Aaron the High Priest must wear a breastplate, robe, fringed tunic, headdress, and a sash. Is that true?

ANNOUNCER: That is correct. This is what was ordered by Moses. It has fashion circles gasping. Egyptian priests won't be dressing in anything half as fancy.

CALLER 1: With all those things, won't Aaron be hot during the summer?

ANNOUNCER: Yes, he will be very hot. Next caller.

CALLER 2: I've heard that Aaron's breastplate will contain twelve precious jewels, representing the twelve tribes, with gold and all kinds of fancy things. Isn't that a bit much to be fashionable?

ANNOUNCER: You might imagine that it would be, but actually it is a lovely piece of work. You'll have to see it yourself when Aaron and his sons are officially anointed as priests.

* * *

MOSES: Preparing for making Aaron and his sons priests is tiring work. Where is my secretary?

SECRETARY: Here. Sorry I'm late. I went to the hairdressers and everyone is getting their hair done for the ceremony. They ran out of hairspray while I was there.

MOSES: Hairspray?

SECRETARY: If the ceremony is going to last seven days, so must our hairdo's.

MOSES: Let's go over the checklist that God discussed with me on Mount Sinai.

SECRETARY: I've called the caterers. The big papers will all be there. The *Canaan Caller*, the *Egyptian Herald*, and the *Israelite Times*. I've checked with the builders and the Ark will be ready tomorrow. The altar needs a little more work.

MOSES: What about the rams and bulls for sacrifices?

SECRETARY: The caterers are taking care of that, too.

MOSES: Remember to tell everyone that the sacrifices are holy and only the priests can eat them.

SECRETARY: This is going to be the social event of the season!

* * *

GOD: Moses, wake up.

MOSES: It isn't morning yet, is it?

GOD: Yes, and it's time to go on with the laws. We finished talking about Aaron and the ceremony to make him a priest. Let's talk about incense. A holy place should not only look good, it should smell good.

MOSES: I was thinking about that myself.

GOD: You should make an altar for burning nice smelling incense. Use gold and . . .

MOSES: Acacia wood?

GOD: Acacia wood. Aaron shall burn incense every morning. A sprinkle a day will keep the odor away. In the evening, he should do it again.

MOSES: Everything will be perfect!

GOD: Could it be any other way?

Ki Tisa

CAST
MOSES
GOD
NARRATOR
MAN
WOMAN 1
AARON
WOMAN 2
JOSHUA

MOSES: How long have I been up here?

GOD: It's been awhile. Why do you ask?

MOSES: I just wonder what everybody is doing down there while they wait for us to finish up.

GOD: They are waiting just where you left them. Back to business. Take a census of everyone. I want you to collect taxes, half a skekel, from everyone over twenty.

MOSES: Taxes? Oy, the Children of Israel are going to love that.

GOD: A half shekel, no more, no less. The money shall go toward building and maintaining the Tent of Meeting and the Ark. Bezalel from the tribe of Judah is the perfect artisan, and Oholiab of the tribe of Dan will be a fine associate. They will do an excellent job of supervising every detail.

MOSES: I'll hurry them along as soon as I get back down there.

GOD: One last thing. Make sure the Israelite people keep My Sabbath, because it is a sign between Me and you forever. Six days you shall work, but the Sabbath will be holy.

NARRATOR: When God finished speaking, Moses was given the two stone tablets inscribed with the finger of God. Meanwhile, down below . . .

* * *

MAN: Yo, Aaron! We've been standing here for almost forty days. I'm beginning to get a little impatient.

WOMAN 1: This waiting around is killing me. What is Moses doing up there?

AARON: Settle down. Moses should be coming down the mountain soon.

WOMAN 2: Wrong, Aaron! Moses is gone. He's dead or vanished. He's never coming back.

ALL: Make us a god who will go before us since Moses, who brought us out from Egypt, has disappeared.

AARON: It is wrong to make a god!

MAN: Aaron, we're not trying to pressure you, but there are 600,000 people that have been standing here for a long time. They are hot and very easily upset. They want a god. Look at them. Do they look friendly? 600,000 to one. Think about it.

AARON: Bring me your gold earrings and I will make a golden calf. Tomorrow at this time we shall celebrate.

ALL: This is your god, oh Israel, which brought you out of Egypt. Let's eat, drink, and be merry! It's party time!

* * *

GOD: Moses, I think you have a problem. Remember the people whom you led out of Egypt?

MOSES: It's been a while. Why?

GOD: They have been quick to turn from Me. They have made a golden calf and are sacrificing to it. Go down to them, for I am going to destroy them.

MOSES: No! What will the Egyptians say? "Look, God brought these slaves out of Egypt to destroy them in the desert." That will not look very good. And what about your promise to Abraham, Isaac, and Jacob?

GOD: But these people have become disloyal, stubborn fools!

MOSES: You swore to make them numerous and give them a land.

GOD: Because of that, I will not destroy them.

NARRATOR: Thereupon, Moses turned and went down from the mountain carrying the two tablets which were written by God — inscribed on both surfaces.

JOSHUA: Moses, you return! And none too soon. It sounds like war down there.

MOSES: No, Joshua. It sounds like singing in the camp.

NARRATOR: Moses saw the golden calf, and the dancing, and he became enraged. He hurled the tablets from his hands and shattered them at the foot of the mountain. He took the calf that they had made and burned it, and ground it up, and threw it into the water, and made Israel drink it.

MAN: Feh. I never drank an earring before. Boy, is Moses angry.

MOSES: Whoever is for the Almighty, come here!

NARRATOR: And all the Levites rallied around him. They took their swords against the rebels. Three thousand people died that day.

MOSES: Listen everybody. You have really done it this time. All I asked was a little patience. God sends plagues and still you don't believe. Then God parts the sea and still you doubt and complain. Well, this is going too far!

JOSHUA: Moses, calm down. Take some aspirin.

MOSES: I've already had two tablets today. You made me break them. Because of this sin, none of you will live to see the Promised Land. It will be for your children. Now, stay put. I shall return.

* * *

GOD: Moses, you have done well. I have singled you out by name.

MOSES: Then let me behold Your presence.

GOD: You cannot see My face, for no one can see Me and live. Sit on that rock and as My presence passes, I will shield you, as it were, with My hand. Then I will take My hand away and you will see My back.

NARRATOR: God then commanded Moses to return to Mount Sinai.

MOSES: *(To the people.)* I am leaving now. What are you all going to do?

MAN: We are going to wait.

MOSES: How long?

MAN: However long it takes. We've learned our lesson. So take your time. If you stop to smell the flowers on the way down, well that's all right, too.

MOSES: I think you've got it.

NARRATOR: So Moses carved two tablets of stone just like the first ones. God came down in a cloud and Moses bowed low to the ground.

GOD: I am ready to make a covenant. Clear the new land of idols.

MOSES: Check.

GOD: Don't make any molten gods.

MOSES: You can count on it.

GOD: Observe Passover, and all firstborn males are to serve Me.

MOSES: Very reasonable.

GOD: Six days you shall work. On the seventh you rest. Observe the Feast of Weeks and the Feast of Ingathering.

MOSES: Roger.

GOD: Don't boil a kid in its mother's milk.

MOSES: Got it. Well, that's it. Forty days and forty nights. Have tablets, will travel. Hey, why is everyone wearing sunglasses?

AARON: Moses, your face is so radiant. It's bright and hard to look at. It's sending forth beams of light!

NARRATOR: And when Moses had finished speaking, he put a veil on his face. When Moses went in before God to speak, he would leave off his veil and when he came out the Israelites would see how radiant the skin of Moses was.

Vayakhel

EXODUS 35:1-38:20

CAST
NARRATOR
MOSES
ISRAELITE 1
ISRAELITE 2
ISRAELITE 3
BEZALEL
OHOLIAB
SECRETARY

NARRATOR: And Moses gathered the whole Israelite community and said to them . . .

MOSES: God has commanded you to observe the seventh day as a Sabbath of complete rest. Don't kindle any fire on the Sabbath day.

ISRAELITE 1: But how will we see at night?

MOSES: Huh?

ISRAELITE 2: Without fire we'll be in darkness — and it will be cold.

MOSES: You have a point. Off the record, why don't you light the fire before Sabbath begins?

ISRAELITE 3: Now, that's a good idea.

MOSES: And now, anyone whose heart so moves them, shall bring gifts to God for the building of the Tabernacle and the Ark.

ISRAELITE 2: I've got some paint brushes.

ISRAELITE 3: You can have my stapler.

MOSES: Actually, I was thinking more along the lines of acacia wood, gold, silver, fine linen, goat's hair, ram's skin, oil, and spices.

ISRAELITE 1: Is this an order?

MOSES: Of course not. It's purely voluntary. Although, if I were asked to offer a gift to the Almighty One above who split the sea, sent ten plagues, and gives bread from the heavens, I think I'd volunteer a nice gift.

BEZALEL: Excuse me, Moses. I got word that you wanted to see me.

OHOLIAB: Same here. My son told me: Moses requests your presence. Be there and don't be square.

MOSES: Your son is getting carried away again. God has endowed you with a special spirit of skill and ability in crafts.

OHOLIAB: I always got A's in Arts and Crafts.

BEZALEL: Me, too. And two years ago I was elected best desert artisan.

OHOLIAB: Me, too. What tribe are you from?

BEZALEL: Judah. Where are you from?

OHOLIAB: Dan — the best tribe in the nation.

BEZALEL: Oh yeah?

OHOLIAB: Yeah!

MOSES: Gentlemen! God has singled you out by name to construct the Tabernacle. Now is the time for peace and cooperation. Come on.

BOTH: Okay.

SECRETARY: Moses, may I speak to you for a moment? Oh, hi, boys!

MOSES: I'm very busy.

SECRETARY: I can see that you are getting worked up again. You know how Jethro said to take it easy. I'm going to warm you up some goat milk. But I should warn you . . . there's a problem with the gifts from the people.

MOSES: So they won't give to God — what a stiff-necked people! I'm going out there and give them a piece of my mind. Hey, the tent opening is shut.

SECRETARY: That's because the people are bringing everything. They really got carried away. They're piling up gold, silver, linens, and gobs of stuff!

MOSES: As I was saying, the Israelites can be a wonderful people. Make a public announcement to stop bringing gifts. We have enough.

SECRETARY: Hey out there! No more gifts! We're going to suffocate!

MOSES: That was very subtle.

* * *

NARRATOR: Then all the skilled artisans began the work of making the Tabernacle.

MOSES: Bezalel, everything looks great.

BEZALEL: Well, the cloth of blue, crimson, and purple yarn is ready. We had a little trouble with the gold loops used for hanging. Someone grabbed an earring without looking.

MOSES: So?

BEZALEL: The earring was in someone's ear at the time. You should have heard the commotion! Other than that, things are going smoothly.

ISRAELITE 1: Bezalel, the Ark is done. The acacia wood is ready for the gold covering.

BEZALEL: We're really cooking. How about the table and the *menorah* for the inside of the Tent?

ISRAELITE 2: We're working on it. But right now, we're on a lunch break.

BEZALEL: Over here are the two altars, one for sacrifices and one for burning incense.

ISRAELITE 1: There's an inscription on the altar.

ISRAELITE 2: It's nothing . . .

ISRAELITE 1: It says . . . Baruch loves Bernice?

BEZALEL: Get rid of that! This is a holy altar.

MOSES: The colors, the hangings, the pillars, everything looks just right.

Pikuday

פְּקוּדֵי

EXODUS 38:21-40:38

CAST
BEZALEL
MOSES
GOD
NARRATOR

BEZALEL: Moses? May I come in?

MOSES: I'm kind of busy right now.

BEZALEL: It's very important. Everything is done.

MOSES: The Tabernacle?

BEZALEL: Complete.

MOSES: The Ark?

BEZALEL: Finished.

MOSES: The entire Tent of Meeting?

BEZALEL: Ready to go.

MOSES: All the furniture and the altars?

BEZALEL: Done.

MOSES: The holy clothes for the priesthood?

BEZALEL: Including the breastplate with twelve precious jewels and lots of gold. The ephod, miter, belt . . . the whole nine yards.

MOSES: Bezalel, it looks great!

BEZALEL: Do I have to remove the Bezalel Construction Company signs just yet?

GOD: Moses, may I have a word with you? This is the God of Israel. I know all the work on My sanctuary is complete.

MOSES: It's truly beautiful. It's a dream come true!

GOD: Yes. Now it's time to arrange the inside properly. Put the furniture in place, and straighten up.

MOSES: Are we ready to install Aaron as High Priest?

GOD: That's right. It shall be done on the first day of the first month.

NARRATOR: In the first month of the second year, on the first of the month, the Tabernacle was set up. Moses took the two tablets and placed them in the Ark, and brought the Ark inside the Tabernacle. He offered up sacrifices and when Moses completed his work, a cloud covered the Tent.

GOD: I'm here.

MOSES: I can't enter the Tent because of the cloud.

GOD: That's for privacy. As long as My presence is with you a cloud will cover the Tent by day and fire will appear by night.

MOSES: All of Israel will see it and know You are in our midst.

GOD: That's the idea.

NARRATOR: When the cloud lifted from the Tabernacle, the Israelites would set out on their journey, but if it did not lift, they would wait. For over the Tabernacle, a cloud of God rested by day, and a fire would appear by night throughout all their journeys.

ALL: This concludes the Book of Exodus. *Chazak, chazak, v'nitchazayk* — be strong, be strong, and let us be strengthened.

Vayikra

ויקרא

LEVITICUS 1:1-5:26

CAST
PERSON 1
PERSON 2
PERSON 3
PERSON 4
NARRATOR
COW
SHEEP
GOD
MOSES
BULL
GOAT

PERSON 1: Did you get your script for the Torah portion of the week?

PERSON 2: I sure did. It's just your luck to have to read *Vayikra*.

PERSON 3: It's been unanimously voted the most boring, unlively book in the Torah.

PERSON 4: You shouldn't all be so negative. *Vayikra* is what you make of it.

PERSON 1: The whole book is about sacrifices and laws!

PERSON 2: Those are not exactly the most fascinating topics to put into a drama.

PERSON 4: Places, everyone! Lights, costumes, cue cards, scripts, props, altar, animals . . . Action!

NARRATOR: When we last left off, the Children of Israel were wandering in the desert after a somewhat messy encounter with the Egyptians, who are now all washed up, so to speak. We have completed the book of Exodus and now are beginning the book of Leviticus, known as *Vayikra*. We start with the first *Sedra*, also known as *Vayikra*.

PERSON 3: Are those animals ready backstage? The Narrator is almost through.

COW: Moo. Where are they taking us?

SHEEP: Baa. How should I know? I received a call last night at 11:00. My agent said to be down here today for an easy job.

NARRATOR: God has called Moses into the Tent of Meeting to explain to him the rules concerning sacrifices. Let's listen in.

GOD: Moses, did you write down everything that I told you?

MOSES: Yes, Holy One, Blessed be You. But we have a lot of sticky details here. Why do we need all these sacrifices?

GOD: Sacrificing animals is a way for the people to show their thanks or to ask for forgiveness. By giving of their own personal property, they show their sincerity.

MOSES: Suppose the whole community of Israel sinned — what would they have to sacrifice?

GOD: Bull.

MOSES: No, I'm not kidding. They could all make a mistake.

GOD: And I've answered you. They sacrifice a bull.

PERSON 1: Backstage! Bring out the bull!

BULL: It's about time — I've been cooped up back here with goats, sheep, and rams. Worst of all, there are turtledoves flying overhead. Where are we going? What are my lines? This is my very first play. Until now, all I've done is commercials.

PERSON 2: If you could just lie on the altar, Mr. Bull, that would be perfect.

BULL: Okay, now what?

PERSON 2: We sacrifice you as a guilt offering.

BULL: Sacrifice? Did you say sacrifice? I want out of my contract! This could ruin my career. Don't I at least get a last meal?

MOSES: God, what if a leader sins before you?

GOD: Then a male goat is sacrificed.

PERSON 3: Bring out the male goat!

GOAT: May I please see the script?

PERSON 3: You won't need one, Sir.

GOAT: Just call me Billy, if you don't mind. Hey, what are you doing?

PERSON 3: We're checking you for blemishes.

GOAT: Blemishes? I do not have a single mark on my body!

PERSON 3: Perfect.

GOAT: Why are you looking?

PERSON 3: According to the law, only unblemished animals can be sacrificed to God. Congratulations, Billy!

GOAT: Sacrificed? Unfair! I want to call the Humane Society! And you can call me Mr. Goat.

MOSES: God, what if an ordinary, run of the mill, camel-riding Israelite sins?

GOD: Then a she-goat or a sheep must be sacrificed. This will clear a person of guilt.

MOSES: And how does someone become guilty?

NARRATOR: Good evening. Have you recently come across some information that is important to courtroom proceedings and failed to step forward? Have you recently touched an unclean thing? Have you uttered an oath and then forgotten that you did so? Well, then, you are in trouble.

PERSON 4: Gracious, what do I do? I didn't speak up in court!

PERSON 3: Dear me, I touched an unclean thing!

PERSON 2: Mercy, I forgot I uttered an oath!

NARRATOR: Sound familiar? Then you need the help of Aaron and sons. The priests will accept your she-goats or turtledoves as sacrifice to God. We're open three times each day, four on the Sabbath and the festivals.

MOSES: God, what if someone deceives a neighbor through robbery or fraud?

GOD: It is required that the money be repaid, plus an extra fifth of the money added to compensate.

MOSES: What if . . .

GOD: What if, what if, what if? Moses, that's enough for today. For someone with a speech problem, you do ask a lot of questions!

PERSON 1: Good — that's a wrap! But we're going to need some more animals for next week.

Tzav

CAST
PORTER
AARON
MOSES
ELIEZER
NARRATOR

PORTER: Excuse me, is this the holy Tabernacle?

AARON: It sure is.

PORTER: I have a delivery order for Moses.

AARON: I'm his brother. I'll sign.

PORTER: Can I enter the Tent?

AARON: I don't advise it. It's only safe to enter if you're a priest.

PORTER: I'll stay out here. I'm no priest.

AARON: What am I signing for?

PORTER: You just bought a whole bunch of incense.

AARON: Great! We need it for our worship services.

PORTER: Whatever you say. Gotta go.

MOSES: Aaron, are you dressed yet?

AARON: You're rushing me!

MOSES: The ceremony to make you High Priest is today. I just want you to be there when we start. Do you know the names of all the sacrifices?

AARON: There are the following types of sacrifices: guilt offering . . .

MOSES: We get a lot of those.

AARON: There's also the sin offering, the meal offering, the thanksgiving offering, and the burnt offering.

MOSES: Very good. Now we can go. I told your sons to meet us there.

* * *

AARON: Hi, sons. Are you excited about becoming priests?

ELIEZER: Yes and no. I like being a priest, but don't you think that seven days is a little long for a ceremony?

MOSES: Those are the rules. Don't leave the Tent of Meeting for seven days.

ELIEZER: Seven days? Seven whole days? This priestly life is very time consuming!

AARON: It's an investment.

MOSES: I agree. Now here are some last minute notes: Are your priestly garments just right? Does the robe fit?

AARON: Yes.

MOSES: Tunic and belt?

AARON: They fit.

MOSES: Breast plate and headdress?

AARON: Yes and no.

MOSES: No headdress?

AARON: Please. The headdress is heavy and tilts my head. I don't want to wear it. Here, feel how heavy it is.

MOSES: It's God's command to have the headdress worn, and in just this way.

AARON: If God commands it, I can make the sacrifice.

NARRATOR: And Moses made Aaron and his sons holy before the congregation. And he touched them with oil. And the altar and the entire Tabernacle he also made holy. And Moses offered up the first sacrifice. Aaron and his sons remained at the entrance to the Tent of Meeting for seven days.

Shemini

LEVITICUS 9:1-11:47

CAST
MOSES
AARON
NADAB
NARRATOR
GOD
ELIEZER
ABIHU
ITHAMAR
ROSIE
PERSON 1
PERSON 2

MOSES: Aaron, it's the eighth day. You may come out of the Tent.

AARON: My sons and I have been in the Tent of Meeting for seven days, just as God commanded.

MOSES: It's over! The eighth day of the celebration is here. My big brother and his sons will be holy priests after today. I'm so proud of you all!

NADAB: Hey, Pops, I'm bored. Can we get started?

AARON: Now you know why I'm pleased that the week has ended.

MOSES: Your Uncle Moses has everything under control, Nadab.

NADAB: Yippee! I get to be a priest! I get to be a priest!

MOSES: Let the ceremony begin. Bring forth the animals for sacrifice.

AARON: Somebody hold the goat! It's getting away!

NARRATOR: Aaron lifted his hands toward the people after making the sin offering, the burnt offering, and the offering of thanksgiving. Moses and Aaron then went inside the Tent of Meeting.

MOSES: Aaron, things are going great. Did you see the look on your sons' faces when they put their hands on the horns of that ox?

GOD: Moses and Aaron.

AARON: The ceremony is almost over.

GOD: I'm proud of you, Aaron. You're doing well. Now comes forth a fire to consume the sacrifice on the altar.

AARON: Wonderful! Now, brother Moses, let us go and bless the people.

NADAB: How long are Dad and Uncle Moses going to be? I'm bored silly. First seven days, and now more waiting. I'm going to have a drink.

ELIEZER: Nadab, relax. Chill out. Settle down.

NADAB: Knock it off, Eliezer. Dad always liked you better. You're his favorite because you're such a goody-goody.

ELIEZER: Nadab, you've got problems.

NADAB: This is ridiculous. I'm going to take my fire pan and finish the program right now. Are any of my brothers with me?

ABIHU: Yeah, let's do it. Maybe then we can get out and cut loose a bit.

NADAB: Good, Abihu. Let's start this thing. Put the incense in your pan.

ELIEZER: Don't do that! You'll get in trouble!

NADAB: Sure we will.

NARRATOR: Nadab and Abihu, Aaron's sons, offered a strange fire which the Almighty had not asked of them. And a fire came forth from God and consumed them.

AARON: All right, sons. Moses and I are ready to finish.

ITHAMAR: Uh, Dad . . .

AARON: Eliezer, where are Nadab and Abihu? We still have work to do.

ELIEZER: Father, Nadab and Abihu offered strange fire and are dead.

AARON: My sons?

MOSES: Calm down, Aaron. You have to go on. Don't offend God. Those two disobeyed God. Being a priest is a position of honor and it must be treated as such. Your sons showed no respect and were . . . fired. But you must not mourn.

AARON: As priests we are separated from the people.

MOSES: Yes, you must drink no wine and you must pay strict attention to your holy task. The penalty for failing to do so is, as you see, very great.

NARRATOR: And Moses gave instructions concerning animals, birds, all living creatures that move in water, and all creatures that swarm on earth. A distinction must be made between the clean and the unclean, between what may be eaten and what may not be eaten.

* * *

ROSIE: Hello there. Welcome to the Desert Diner. Can I get you some goat milk before dinner?

PERSON 1: Thanks, Rosie. We'd love some.

PERSON 2: I'll take a swine sandwich.

ROSIE: Sorry, remember the rules. We have some restrictions. The management only serves animals with cleft hooves that chew their cud.

PERSON 2: What about a vulture salad?

ROSIE: No birds of prey can be served. But we do have some lovely braised quail tips, or roasted breast of turtledove.

PERSON 1: How about the Lizard Supreme?

ROSIE: Nope. Lizards, crocodiles, chameleons, and moles are off limits.

PERSON 1: Okay. I'll have the cow steak with palm hearts.

ROSIE: Sorry. You just drank goat's milk. Can't mix it with meat.

PERSON 1: Then I guess I'll have the peanut butter sandwich.

PERSON 2: Me too.

Tazriya

תַזְרִיעַ

LEVITICUS 12:1-13:59

CAST
NURSE
DOCTOR
PATIENT 1
PATIENT 2
PATIENT 3
PRIEST

NURSE: Doctor, there are twenty-five more people in the waiting tent. Will they get to see you today?

DOCTOR: I don't know. These new laws that God gave Moses and Aaron are really shaking people up.

NURSE: Everybody thinks they have leprosy.

DOCTOR: I can understand why they want to separate lepers from the general population, but everybody is scared. Can we send some of these people to the clinic in the territory of Reuven or Judah?

NURSE: I'm sorry, doctor. All the clinics are mobbed.

DOCTOR: Very well. Bring in the next one.

PATIENT 1: Hi doc. When I heard the new law, I thought I better see you. I have this white swelling on my arm.

DOCTOR: That sure is a white swelling. But the hair hasn't turned white, and there is not a single trace of discoloration. You're okay. Next!

PATIENT 2: Doctor, I have this white swelling with some red streaks in it.

DOCTOR: You sure do. Stay here a minute.

NURSE: Did you ring?

DOCTOR: Yes. I don't want to alarm the patient, but I think she has leprosy. Be very subtle when you come over to us. Write her a pass to go see a priest.

PATIENT 2: What's the verdict? Am I clean?

DOCTOR: I can't say. I want to send you to a priest who will inspect you more closely.

NURSE: Here's the pass, doctor. Can I see that swelling? Yich. So that's what leprosy looks like. It's horrible!

DOCTOR: Thank you, Nurse! That was very subtle. Now please bring some water for the patient. We'll try to revive her.

NURSE: Sorry. Do you want to see some bald people?

DOCTOR: Yes! Bald heads are the easiest ones to inspect.

PATIENT 3: What are you looking for?

DOCTOR: I'm looking for white infections and scaling.

PATIENT 3: What if somebody has it?

DOCTOR: He or she is unclean and has to go live with other lepers. We have a whole leper colony.

NURSE: Doctor, Look at all those baldies! They look like a mountain range when they're lined up like that.

DOCTOR: Meet my nurse. She's very discreet and always knows just the right thing to say.

PRIEST: As for the person with a leprous infection, his clothes shall be torn, his head left bare, and he shall cover over his upper lip, and he shall call out "Unclean! Unclean!" He shall be unclean as long as the disease is on him. Being unclean, he shall dwell apart; his dwelling shall be outside the camp.

Metzora

LEVITICUS 14:1-15:33

CAST
BOY
GIRL
MOTHER
DAD
NARRATOR
PRIEST
OWNER

BOY: I am so excited! We're going to see Dad again.

GIRL: It's been two years since he came down with that dreaded disease called leprosy.

MOTHER: You know, children, I didn't know if we'd ever be together again. This is so wonderful!

BOY: Mom, don't cry.

GIRL: I almost forgot what he looks like.

DAD: Is anyone home?

BOY: We sure are!

MOTHER: Honey, it's so good to see you! You look . . .

GIRL: Bald!

BOY: Dad, what happened to your hair?

GIRL: And your beard is gone.

MOTHER: And what happened to your eyebrows? You're a hairless wonder!

DAD: It's all part of the cleansing ceremony. A person who is cured of leprosy has to be shaven and offer sacrifices. I was kept in isolation for seven days to make sure that I was really healed.

MOTHER: Well, welcome home, baldy!

* * *

NARRATOR: Meanwhile . . .

PRIEST: Knock knock. Building inspector.

OWNER: Who's there? Oh, it's a Levite. Can I help you?

PRIEST: I have a complaint from some neighbors that this house has leprosy.

OWNER: The house? No way. How can a house have leprosy?

PRIEST: Germs, Mr. House Owner. Little infectious bugs. God commanded Moses and Aaron regarding houses with leprosy.

OWNER: I don't believe you.

PRIEST: Read the book, Mister. Leviticus, Chapter 14. Stand aside.

OWNER: I object!

PRIEST: What is this greenish and reddish streak on the wall?

OWNER: It's last night's dinner, I swear.

PRIEST: They go deep into the wall. This house is condemned.

OWNER: What did I do wrong?

PRIEST: I don't know. Leprosy is an ugly business. It strikes anywhere and anyone from the tallest person to the most innocent two-story office tent.

Acharay Mot

אַחֲרֵי מוֹת

LEVITICUS 16:1-18:30

CAST
NARRATOR
GOD
MOSES
AARON
GOAT 1
GOAT 2

NARRATOR: God spoke to Moses after the death of the two sons of Aaron, who died when they drew near before the Lord.

GOD: Moses, I have some information for you to pass on to Aaron.

MOSES: What should I tell him?

GOD: I don't want Aaron in the Holy of Holies all the time. It's to be a private place, and he shouldn't treat it like a family room. Once a year is enough.

MOSES: Only once a year?

GOD: He can collect everyone's sins for a year and then he can come in and ask for atonement.

MOSES: Anything else?

GOD: Have him wear his special linen clothes when he visits. It's also appropriate that he bathe before dressing. As a matter of fact, we can make it a day of atonement for everybody.

MOSES: When?

GOD: The tenth day of the seventh month.

MOSES: Restrictions? We'll have to have them if this is going to be a special day.

GOD: No one may work. Everyone will practice self-denial and atone for their sins.

MOSES: Very good. I'll send out a memo tomorrow.

* * *

AARON: Moses, have you seen my *Sinai Sports Illustrated*? I was right in the middle of this exposé on camel racing.

MOSES: No, I haven't seen it.

AARON: I might have left it in the Holy of Holies. I'll go check.

MOSES: Aaron, God has prohibited you from entering there except on the Day of Atonement. Here's the memo.

AARON: But . . . but . . .

* * *

GOAT 1: Hey, do you know what's going on here?

GOAT 2: I sure don't. There I was, minding my own business, grazing like a good little goat, and all of a sudden, swoosh, they grabbed me.

GOAT 1: Same with me. Look at all these people. Isn't that Aaron over there? He looks different. He's not wearing his everyday priest clothes.

GOAT 2: This must be some special type of ceremony.

GOAT 1: So why are we here?

GOAT 2: I don't know. Maybe we're the entertainment for the kiddies.

AARON: Behold, you see two goats.

GOAT 2: Hey, he's talking about us! Quit wagging your tail.

AARON: They are both clean animals with no blemish.

GOAT 1: You're darn tootin'. I pride myself on good grooming.

AARON: One shall be killed as a sin sacrifice, and the other shall be given all the sins of Israel and be sent out into the wilderness.

GOAT 2: Did you hear what he just said?

GOAT 1: I heard it, but I don't believe it! What kind of holiday is this, anyway? Listen, I'll go into the wilderness.

GOAT 2: No, no. You stay here, I'll go.

NARRATOR: And Aaron offered a goat as a sin offering, and he laid his hand on the live goat and confessed all of Israel's sins, and the goat was set free in the wilderness.

* * *

GOD: Moses, I have a few more words to say.

MOSES: Let me get my notebook.

GOD: I've been watching the people. Draw up a list of rules about who people can marry. I don't want parents marrying their children, brothers marrying sisters . . .

MOSES: Check. I sure wouldn't want to marry Miriam.

GOD: It's important that people don't marry their relatives. There are too many problems.

MOSES: Good point.

GOD: Just make sure everyone gets the message.

MOSES: You can count on it.

Kedoshim קְדוֹשִׁים

LEVITICUS 19:1-20:27

CAST
GOD
MOSES
ANNOUNCER
JUDGE 1
JUDGE 2
JUDGE 3

GOD: Moses, do you have everything? Your notes, your books, your charts?

MOSES: I think so. I'm very nervous. I hate talking to the annual Biblical Judges Convention.

GOD: There are a lot of laws for them to learn. But first, tell the whole Israelite community that they must become a holy people, because I the Almighty your God am holy.

MOSES: That's a very good thought. I'll use it.

ANNOUNCER: Judges, please rise for the honorable Chief Judge of Israel, Moses son of Amram!

MOSES: Thank you. Let us start with some new laws that will now go into effect.

JUDGE 1: Could I interrupt for a moment?

MOSES: I haven't started yet.

JUDGE 1: I want to speak out on an issue that concerns us all.

MOSES: Very well.

JUDGE 1: About our salary . . .

JUDGE 2: A few shekels a day is nothing! We want more.

JUDGE 3: And chauffeur driven camels.

MOSES: Hold it! Settle down. You are supposed to be judges. This is a session on new laws.

JUDGE 2: Then let's make new laws that judges get raises . . .

JUDGE 3: . . . and chauffeur driven camels.

MOSES: Enough! Now, let us begin. Revere your mother and father, and observe Shabbat. Don't make idols; don't steal; be sure to leave food in the field for the poor; don't insult the deaf or put stumbling blocks in front of the blind.

JUDGE 1: These are good laws. They make a lot of sense.

MOSES: Here are a few more. Don't make cloth from two types of material, and don't cut the corners of your beards.

JUDGE 2: Why not?

MOSES: Because.

JUDGE 2: Because why?

MOSES: Because God said so.

JUDGE 2: Why?

MOSES: Because we're not supposed to be exactly like everyone else. We are going to a special land, and we have to act special.

JUDGE 2: Oh.

MOSES: Don't treat strangers badly. We were once strangers in Egypt. And there will be no wizardry.

JUDGE 3: There goes my second job.

MOSES: A man can't marry his mother or sister or daughter.

JUDGE 1: What happens if one does?

MOSES: He shall be put to death.

JUDGE 1: That could be a deterrent.

MOSES: I close with God's words: I am your God, who has set you apart from other peoples. You shall be holy to Me, for I the Almighty am holy.

Emor

אֱמוֹר

LEVITICUS 21:1-24:23

CAST
AARON
PRIEST 1
PRIEST 2
SALESGIRL
MOSES
PERSON
HALF-ISRAELITE
ISRAELITE

AARON: As the High Priest, I have decided to call this meeting of all the priests in order to clear up a few things.

PRIEST 1: Can you make it quick? I've got to do three sin offerings and a guilt sacrifice this morning.

AARON: I want to make sure that you know what this job entails. A priest cannot go near a dead person, except for close relatives. A priest can't shave smooth any part of his head.

PRIEST 2: My barber is going to love that.

AARON: A priest cannot marry a woman who has been married before. And why is this so?

PRIEST 1: I don't know.

AARON: Because we are holy. Who is holy?

PRIESTS: We are!

AARON: Why are we holy?

PRIESTS: Because we serve God!

AARON: Good. Meeting adjourned.

* * *

SALESGIRL: Can I help you, Sir?

MOSES: My name is Moses.

SALESGIRL: Oh, wow! It's really you! The guy with the miracles! The big cheese himself! What would you like?

MOSES: I have a custom order.

SALESGIRL: Let me get a note pad. Meanwhile, browse through our cards. There is a great little card to send to a kid who gets his first donkey.

MOSES: I need a calendar. God gave me dates for new holidays, so it's time we produced a calendar.

SALESGIRL: What are the dates?

MOSES: First is the Sabbath. That comes every seventh day. Then in the first month on the fourteenth day begins the Feast of Unleavened Bread.

SALESGIRL: That's a great holiday. I love *matzah*.

MOSES: Seven weeks later is the harvest festival. Then on the first day of the seventh month is the New Year, a sacred occasion commemorated by loud blasts of the horns.

SALESGIRL: Did you say that you wanted the New Year to start in the seventh month? Isn't that a bit odd?

MOSES: Yes, it does seem strange. Perhaps you would like to challenge God on this issue?

SALESGIRL: No, thanks. I know what happened to Pharaoh.

MOSES: Also, color in the tenth day of the seventh month as the Day of Atonement, and the fifteenth as the beginning of the Feast of Booths.

* * *

PERSON: Moses, I'm glad I found you. There's a fight going on outside! One guy is an Israelite and the other is a half-Israelite on his mother's side.

MOSES: Hey, you two, break it up!

HALF-ISRAELITE: I'll stop only if he gets off me and stops pounding my head into the ground.

MOSES: Sounds reasonable. Let him go. What seems to be the problem?

PERSON: They were fighting over something they both saw. But the half-Israelite used God's name in vain.

HALF-ISRAELITE: It was a slip of the tongue. I got angry.

MOSES: You broke one of the Commandments.

HALF-ISRAELITE: But it didn't hurt anybody.

PERSON: You broke one of the Commandments.

HALF-ISRAELITE: You're upset, aren't you?

ISRAELITE: You broke one of the Commandments.

HALF-ISRAELITE: I guess that was a silly thing to do. Go ahead, punish me. Beat me. Whip me. Throw me in a pit.

ISRAELITE: The punishment is to be stoned to death.

HALF-ISRAELITE: You guys are serious. How about if I apologize?

MOSES: God has ordered that you be stoned. Let this be a lesson to those who break the Commandments.

PERSON: Any last words?

HALF-ISRAELITE: Is there any wiggle room here? Do you take bribes? Can we negotiate?

Behar

CAST
GOD
MOSES
ISRAELITE 1
ISRAELITE 2

GOD: Moses, wake up! I have a wonderful idea.

MOSES: I hope so. It's three o'clock in the morning.

GOD: Put this down in the book.

MOSES: Okay. What idea is it?

GOD: *Sh'mitah.*

MOSES: *Gezundheit.*

GOD: That's not a sneeze, that's the wonderful idea!

MOSES: Huh?

GOD: You'll love it. The labor unions will go bananas!

MOSES: I don't understand what you're talking about.

GOD: Let Me explain. So far, everybody enjoys the Sabbath as a day of rest.

MOSES: That's very true.

GOD: *Sh'mitah* is a rest year!

MOSES: A whole year?

GOD: Sometimes, an idea hits You, and bam! It's one of My best laws. *Sh'mitah* will be a rest year for the land. Every seventh year, the land will not be plowed or planted.

MOSES: How will we eat?

GOD: Moses, trust Me. I'll bless the sixth year with extra bounty.

MOSES: Can You do that?

GOD: Did I split the Sea of Reeds?

MOSES: Well, if You want *Sh'mitah,* You've got it. Can we eat of whatever the land produces during the Sabbath year?

GOD: You and your servants and your animals may eat anything that grows by itself on the land.

* * *

ISRAELITE 1: Did you read the new law about *Sh'mitah*?

ISRAELITE 2: I sure did. That is one far out idea! No farming every seventh year. Talk about vacation time off!

ISRAELITE 1: And did you read about the Jubilee Year?

ISRAELITE 2: No, I skipped right to the battle reports.

ISRAELITE 1: Every fifty years, the land goes back to the original owners. All servants are released, and the lands gets a rest.

ISRAELITE 2: *Sh'mitah*, Jubilee Year, and Sabbath. This is turning into a great little religion. We get more work benefits than anyone else!

ISRAELITE 1: *Sh'mitah!* . . .

ISRAELITE 2: What about it?

ISRAELITE 1: Nothing. I was just sneezing!

Bechukotai   בְּחֻקֹּתַי

LEVITICUS 26:3-27:34

CAST
ISRAELITE 1
ISRAELITE 2
ISRAELITE 3
NARRATOR
ANNOUNCER
PERSON 1
PERSON 2
PERSON 3
PERSON 4

ISRAELITE 1: Hey everyone, I just heard about the latest commandments that Moses discussed. There's some good stuff in here.

ISRAELITE 2: If it's more laws about sacrifices or priests, I don't want to hear it. All Moses seems to talk about are those two topics.

ISRAELITE 3: Quit picking on Moses. It's not easy to find new sermons every day.

NARRATOR: God said: If you follow My laws and faithfully observe My commandments, I'll grant you rains so that the earth will yield its produce and the trees of the field their fruit.

ISRAELITE 1: There are other good things that will happen if we listen to God. There will be peace. We will be fruitful, and we will multiply, and there will be loads of food.

ISRAELITE 3: It sounds pretty good. Sign me up!

ISRAELITE 2: I'm not sure. It's hard to be good. What happens if Israelites don't listen to God's law?

ANNOUNCER: Hi, there. Are you tired of following rules? Do you want to do whatever you please? Not a good idea! But now there's instant relief. The Kol Ra Clinic can get rid of those little voices crying out, "Do bad things." Here's how we work. First we visit some people who disobeyed the commandments. Hello.

PERSON 1: Go away.

ANNOUNCER: Are you an evil person?

PERSON 1: Yeah. I'm rotten.

ANNOUNCER: Tell everyone what happened to you.

PERSON 1: I used to do a lot of sneaky things, like yank on tent ropes and run. Then, suddenly, God sends pestilence and fever and I don't feel so hot. My land stopped giving fruit. So I called Kol Ra Clinic, and by obeying God, I'm doing better now.

ANNOUNCER: Here's a whole group of bad people. Tell us what happened to you when you didn't observe God's commandments.

PERSON 2: My city was destroyed.

PERSON 3: Enemies invaded.

PERSON 4: We were forced to flee.

ANNOUNCER: Well, there you have it. blessings or curses — you make the choice. But if you want blessings and find it hard to be good, call the Kol Ra Clinic. We're in the sandy pages.

ISRAELITE 2: So, let me see if I have it right. If we do good and observe God's laws, we're blessed . . .

ISRAELITE 3: But if we disobey God's laws, we're up the Red Sea without a paddle!

ALL: This concludes the Book of Leviticus. *Chazak, chazak, v'nitchazayk* — be strong, be strong, and let us be strengthened.

BaMidbar

NUMBERS 1:1-4:20

CAST
CENSUS TAKER
ELIAB
RIVKA
VOICE
GOD
MOSES
AARON

CENSUS TAKER: Knock, knock! Hello?

ELIAB: Is there someone at the entrance?

CENSUS TAKER: Yoo hoo! Hello! Anyone home?

ELIAB: There IS someone at the door.

CENSUS TAKER: Didn't you hear me knock?

ELIAB: How loud is a knock on a tent?

CENSUS TAKER: Good point. Maybe that's why nobody ever seems to be home.

ELIAB: Come on in and sit down.

CENSUS TAKER: I'm glad you said that. My feet are killing me! I've been pounding the sand for three days.

ELIAB: What for?

CENSUS TAKER: You haven't heard? God commanded Moses to take a census of all clans, listing by name every male over twenty years of age.

ELIAB: Wow, that's some job!

CENSUS TAKER: You can say that again.

ELIAB: Wow, that's some job!

CENSUS TAKER: Let's get started. Name?

ELIAB: Yes.

CENSUS TAKER: Come on. I don't need comedians. Job?

ELIAB: I'm a comedian. I perform nightly at the Camel and Grill.

CENSUS TAKER: Really?

ELIAB: No. Actually, I am the leader of the tribe of Zebulun.

CENSUS TAKER: How many children do you have?

ELIAB: Hmm, that's hard to say. I have ten wives. Hold on. Rivka, how many kids do we have?

RIVKA: Thirty-six.

VOICE: Waah! Waah!

RIVKA: Thirty-seven.

CENSUS TAKER: They must give you a lot of pleasure.

RIVKA: Try getting a baby sitter for thirty-seven kids!

CENSUS TAKER: Eliab, you could help me out a lot. Do you by any chance have a list of everyone in the tribe of Zebulun?

ELIAB: Actually, I do. Here it is. 57,400 names!

CENSUS TAKER: You're a big tribe!

ELIAB: Not as big as Judah or Dan, but we hold our own.

VOICE: Waah! Waah!

ELIAB: Make that thirty-eight.

* * *

GOD: Moses, how is the census going?

MOSES: Terrific! We have 603,550. That doesn't include the tribe of Levi, which You told us not to count. How come?

GOD: I've got some big plans for the Levites.

MOSES: What?

GOD: They will be my special helpers. The tribe of Levi will be in charge of the Tabernacle, all its furnishings and everything that goes with it. They shall tend it, set it up, and take it down.

AARON: Moses, what are you doing here?

MOSES: God has given the tribe of Levi the job of tending the Holy Tabernacle.

AARON: Oh, good. I can't handle this by myself.

MOSES: Now, what happens to the firstborn males who have been serving You? If we have Levites and firstborn males, it's going to get very crowded.

GOD: I shall release the firstborn children from service to Me. Each family may redeem its firstborn son from the priesthood. Each clan of the Levites shall take responsibility for part of the sanctuary.

AARON: I'll let the Levites know the good news.

MOSES: God has told me all the details of each clan's special job. It's very important that they get it right.

AARON: Don't worry. Ithamar, Eliezer, and I will make sure everyone does a good job.

Naso

נָשֹׂא

CAST
MOSES
GERSHON
KOHATH
MERARI
SERVANT
MOTHER
SON
SECRETARY
NARRATOR

MOSES: Settle down, everyone! I want you to remain calm.

GERSHON: I don't understand what Moses is saying. Do you?

KOHATH: Beats me. I think he's trying to ask us to do something. I dunno.

MOSES: Shhh! I have called a meeting of all the leaders of the tribe of Levi to inform you of a major change. Up until now, the firstborn males have been performing certain holy duties. They no longer will be involved.

MERARI: Then who is going to do it? It's very important to have people in the service of God.

MOSES: I'm glad you said that. The Levites have been chosen to take care of the Tabernacle and serve God. The Levites will dismantle the Tabernacle and carry it when we move. You will then set it up and serve in it when we camp.

MERARI: I didn't volunteer. What's the matter with the tribe of Asher? They never have to do anything!

KOHATH: Count me out, too. What a dumb idea!

MOSES: It is God's command.

KOHATH: On the other hand, I could get used to it. The Tabernacle, huh? It's okay with me.

MOSES: I am so glad you see it that way. After all, we certainly wouldn't want to anger the Power that sent ten plagues, split the Sea of Reeds . . .

GERSHON: We get the picture.

MOSES: I need a head count of each of the three clans of Levi. Number the men who are between 20 and 50 years of age. The Gershon clan's assignment is to carry the Tabernacle and the Tent of Meeting.

MERARI: Too bad, Gershon. Look at it this way, it'll keep you in shape.

MOSES: The clan of Merari will carry all the planks and supports for the Tent of Meeting.

GERSHON: Too bad, Merari. But as someone once said, it'll keep you in shape.

MOSES: The Kohathite clan will handle the holy vessels. Congratulations everyone! Please report to Aaron at the Tabernacle for your in-house assignments.

SERVANT: Excuse me, Moses. There's a family outside to see you.

MOTHER: Moses, I am so upset!

SON: Ma, you are embarrassing me!

MOTHER: Shhh. This boy is causing me grief. All the other children are going into nice occupations. Elihu is a shepherd. Dan is a winekeeper. My son wants to be a Nazirite.

MOSES: What is so bad about that? A Nazirite is someone who commits himself to God.

SON: It's my way of thanking God.

MOTHER: A simple thank-you would have done. Look at him! His hair is longer than mine!

SON: A Nazirite may not shave his hair.

MOTHER: Yesterday I had a party and everyone was drinking wine except him.

SON: A Nazirite may not eat or drink anything from grapevines.

MOTHER: Moses, did you hear him? Tell him that he is crazy! Make him listen to his mother. Go ahead, Moses!

MOSES: I think your son is to be commended for wanting to serve God in such a way.

MOTHER: You're a big help! I'm glad I came!

SERVANT: Moses, I'm sorry to bother you again, but your social secretary is here and must see you.

SECRETARY: Moses, you are going to finish the altar tomorrow. Then you will anonit it with oil. When that's done, I thought it would be appropriate to throw a little party to celebrate.

MOSES: That sounds fine. I hope the celebration does not run too late.

SECRETARY: Actually, its a twelve-day affair.

MOSES: Twelve days! I thought you said it was a little something that you were throwing!

SECRETARY: Don't get all worked up. Remember what the doctor said. Here, take these two tablets. We need twelve days — one for each tribe. Otherwise, someone might feel left out.

MOSES: Are we charging anything for this "little" party?

SECRETARY: I suggested a silver bowl weighing 130 shekels, and a silver basin weighing 70 shekels. Also, I asked them to chip in sheep, bulls, lambs, and the usual.

MOSES: That's good.

SECRETARY: Of course it is! Remember to wear something nice. Wear the red robe. It makes you look younger, and it doesn't wrinkle.

NARRATOR: This was the dedication offering for the altar from the leaders of Israel: 12 silver bowls, 12 silver basins, 2,400 sanctuary shekels, and lots and lots of animals.

Beha'alotecha

בְּהַעֲלֹתְךָ

NUMBERS 8:1-12:16

CAST
COHEN
SHIFRA
ABE
ISRAELITE 1
MOSES
ISRAELITE 2
GOD
NARRATOR
MIRIAM
AARON

COHEN: Good evening, and welcome to the nightly news. My name is Dave Cohen here at KSINAI. Our top story tonight is the special ceremony that officially marked the tribe of Levi as a holy tribe. Here's a report from our social editor, Shifra Ben Aminavi.

SHIFRA: Thank you, Dave. This ceremony marked the beginning of Levi's service to God. It was very exciting. Aaron's wife Elishevah was dressed in a charming purple chiffon robe, and Joshua's new camel hide boots were a smash. Lovely *hors d'oeuvres* were served in the late afternoon for invited guests. The colors of the party were gold and . . .

COHEN: Excuse me, Shifra. I hate to interrupt, but this is supposed to be a story about the actual ceremony.

SHIFRA: Dave, you are so boring! Who cares about the fact that the Levites had to cleanse themselves and offer sacrifices and that God formally transferred authority from the firstborn sons to the tribe of Levi? I think the people out there would much rather know that Moses' wife Zipporah had a little rip in her robe. Shifra Ben Aminavi signing off.

COHEN: Let's go now to our weather report. Abe!

ABE: As you well know, a cloud covers the Tabernacle most of the time. In the evening it appears as if on fire. We move to a new place only when God tells us to. When the cloud lifts, it's time to pack the bags. Today the cloud stayed in place and showed no sign of rising, which is good, since I personally am getting tired of *shlepping* around this desert. Packing, unpacking . . .

COHEN: Wait a second, Abe. I've just received a bulletin that the cloud covering the Holy Tabernacle has lifted! All Israelites are to prepare to move out. Dave Cohen signing off.

* * *

ISRAELITE 1: Excuse me, Moses. I have to talk to you.

MOSES: Can it wait? I must attend to the sounding of the silver trumpets.

ISRAELITE 1: But we're hungry!

MOSES: Go outside and collect manna. That's why God sends it.

ISRAELITE 1: We're sick of manna! We get it every day for breakfast and lunch.

ISRAELITE 2: We're hungry and want real food!

MOSES: Who is "we"?

ISRAELITE 2: The people of Israel. Everybody.

MOSES: Out of 600,000 people, not one is satisfied?

ISRAELITE 1: We demand fish. Just like in Egypt.

MOSES: Fish? Where am I going to find fish for 600,000 people? This is a desert! Besides, if we emptied the ocean there wouldn't be enough fish to feed these people!

ISRAELITE 2: We want real food. Meat and potatoes and salads and soft drinks.

ISRAELITE 1: And we want it now!

MOSES: Such patience. I'll be right back. Oh, God, the people want meat. First You care for them as a nurse cares for babies. Then You prepare them for their own land. But is that enough? Nooooo. They want more food, so You send them manna. Is that enough? Nooooo. Now they want meat!

GOD: Meat they shall have. Not just for a day, but for a month. They'll eat it until it is coming out of their noses and it becomes loathsome to them.

MOSES: I hate to throw a damper on things, but we don't have that much meat. This is, after all, not just a little snack.

GOD: Moses, you're thinking like a human. Is there a limit to God's power?

* * *

ISRAELITE 2: Look, the wind of the Almighty is sweeping quail up from the sea! It's real food!

ISRAELITE 1: Thanks, Moses. That's enough quail.

MOSES: More is coming. You'll be eating quail for 30 days.

ISRAELITE 2: But we might get sick of it.

MOSES: No doubt.

* * *

NARRATOR: And God struck the people with a very severe plague. The place was called *Kivrot-HaTa'avah*, because the people who had a craving for meat are buried there.

* * *

MIRIAM: Aaron, we have to talk.

AARON: What's up, Miriam?

MIRIAM: Our little brother Moses has married a Cushite.

AARON: I know that, and so does Moses.

MIRIAM: Cushites are . . . well, different. How could he marry such a woman?

AARON: Maybe Moses loves her.

MIRIAM: Aaron, stop being logical. Shh, here she comes. Hi, honey! It's very daring of you to wear white sandals after Yom Kippur!

AARON: It really was foolish of him to marry her. Maybe we should have a talk with him.

GOD: You think so?

AARON: Who said that?

GOD: Aaron, what are you and Miriam up to?

MIRIAM: We're talking behind Moses' back. He has married a Cushite. Why would he do that?

GOD: Maybe he likes her. Moses hasn't done anything wrong. On the other hand, you have been gossiping. That is uncalled for.

AARON: Oh no! Miriam, your skin is full of scales. You've been punished for gossiping.

MOSES: Hello, all. Aaron you look good. Miriam, you look terrible! Oh, God, I pray — heal her.

GOD: I will, but only after seven days. During that time, she will be shut out from the camp. We shall not move the camp until she returns.

NARRATOR: So Miriam was shut out of the camp for seven days, and the people did not march on until Miriam was readmitted.

Shelach Lecha שְׁלַח לְךָ

NUMBERS 13:1-15:41

CAST
GOD
MOSES
CALEB
JOSHUA
NARRATOR
NAHBI
ISRAELITE
PALTI

GOD: Moses, this is the Almighty.

MOSES: Good morning! It's a beautiful day.

GOD: Thank you, Moses. Send some people to scout the land of Canaan.

MOSES: A spy mission? Ooh, this is exciting! I'll select one person from each tribe.

* * *

CALEB: Moses, I have a question.

MOSES: What is it, Caleb?

CALEB: If this is supposed to be a spy mission, why are practically all the Israelites here to watch us leave?

MOSES: Word must have gotten out.

CALEB: That's an understatement. Look at today's headlines in the *Sinai Sun*; "Spies to Leave on Top Secret Mission To Canaan."

MOSES: Don't worry. Nobody else will find out.

CALEB: Right. After all, 600,000 people can keep a secret as easily as twelve can.

JOSHUA: Moses, I'm worried about some of these spies. Look at Palti of Benjamin. His knees are shaking. And Nahbi of Naphtali is crying in his mother's arms!

MOSES: Joshua and Caleb, stop worrying! Attention, please. I want the attention of all the spies. Gaddiel, enough biting your nails. This is a very important mission. Find out all you can about the country. Good luck. Now go, spy!

* * *

NARRATOR: The spies went up and scouted the land. At the end of forty days they returned from spying out the land. They went straight to Moses and Aaron and the whole community.

MOSES: How was it?

JOSHUA: The land is flowing with milk and honey!

NAHBI: And the people are giants.

CALEB: There is honey and fruit!

NAHBI: And gigantic people who live in huge fortified cities.

JOSHUA: We gathered a single cluster of grapes that takes two men to carry!

NAHBI: And there are these huge, gigantic, monster people that live in fortresses.

ISRAELITE: Why do I get the feeling that these guys were spying in two different places?

PALTI: I know that I can speak for ten of the spies, not including Caleb and Joshua. Let me put it this way. We would look like grasshoppers next to the people of that land. In other words, they'd eat us for dinner!

JOSHUA: Grasshoppers? Monsters? What are you talking about?

CALEB: We can conquer the land!

PALTI: Only if they laugh to death when they see us coming.

ISRAELITE: We should have stayed in Egypt. Moses brought us here to die!

MOSES: There they go again, crying and feeling sorry for themselves. Come on, snap out of it! This is a time for action!

ISRAELITE: I agree — let's have some action. Let's pack it in and return to Egypt!

MOSES: That's no answer. What does that solve?

ISRAELITE: You're right. Instead, let's stone Moses and Aaron. Everyone get ready to throw rocks at them!

* * *

GOD: Moses, what is going on?

MOSES: Oh, God, we have another situation. I am so tired of hearing the same thing over and over . . .

GOD: Are they complaining again?

MOSES: They want to go back to Egypt. Not only that — they want to throw rocks at me!

GOD: That does it. I'm putting an end to these people.

MOSES: God, this is difficult to say. Please, be slow to anger. If You put an end to these people, other nations will say that You were powerless to bring us into the Promised Land.

GOD: All right. I shall not destroy them.

MOSES: Thank God!

GOD: You're welcome.

* * *

MOSES: Your attention, please! God has said that because you keep rebelling, nobody now older than twenty years of age shall enter the Land.

ISRAELITE: Suppose we said that we're sorry?

MOSES: Too late. Nobody except Joshua and Caleb will make it into Canaan. Only those who are now children will live to enter the Land.

NAHBI: What about the rest of the spies? Can we come into the Land?

MOSES: Those who spied the Land and came back with stories that caused people to doubt God shall die of plague.

NAHBI: I guess that's your way of saying that we won't be going into the Land.

MOSES: I think you got the message!

Korach

קֹרַח

CAST
MOSES
KORACH
AARON
ABIRAM
DATHAN
ANNOUNCER
MAN
WOMAN
GOD
NARRATOR
CHIEFTAIN 1
CHIEFTAIN 2
CHIEFTAIN 3

MOSES: Well, Aaron, things are going fairly well right now. The quail are falling from the sky on schedule, the laws are at the printer, and we are out of Egypt. What could go wrong?

KORACH: Moses, come out here please!

AARON: I think that answers your question.

MOSES: Peep through the tent and see who's out there.

AARON: It's Korach, Dathan, and Abiram.

MOSES: I think we can handle them. Anyone else?

AARON: Oh, about 250 other leaders are with them. How are we going to stand up to all those people?

MOSES: It may be a friendly visit.

ABIRAM: Come out with your hands up, you cowards!

AARON: Something tells me this isn't going to be a friendly visit.

KORACH: Moses, you and your brother Aaron have gone too far. Everybody is holy and God is in our midst. But you have raised yourselves above everyone else.

AARON: What have we done? Moses has set aside the whole tribe of Levi to be priests, and you are from Levi. And he set me and my family up as the High Priests, which is only fair because I am his brother.

DATHAN: What's fair about that?

MOSES: Stop bickering. Korach, you think that I've gone too far? Here's what we'll do. We're going to have a contest. Aaron and I against you and your followers.

AARON: Moses, don't get carried away — there are 250 people standing over there! Have you lost your senses? We each take on 125 guys and whoever finishes first can help the other guy? Is that your plan?

MOSES: Relax, Aaron. You're misjudging the situation.

AARON: All these people, leaders of the nation, want to overthrow us and you want to challenge them to hand-to-hand combat? I understand the situation. The desert winds have dried your mind!

MOSES: Korach, it is not us whom you challenge, but God. Therefore, let us be tested together.

KORACH: I and my company accept the challenge.

DATHAN AND ABIRAM: Count us out!

MOSES: Each of us will take a fire pan and put fire in it, along with incense. If God accepts one of the pans, that person will be considered the holy one chosen by God. He will be the High Priest.

AARON: Moses, will you please come inside the Tent for a minute? What is wrong with you? You might be giving them the whole nation!

KORACH: That's acceptable. I'll be there with my men at high noon.

ANNOUNCER: This is Asher Ben Shapiro, standing just outside the arena where a classic confrontation between Moses and the rebels is about to begin. The crowd is gathering, and there seems to be a lot of support growing for Korach and the rebels.

MAN: Boo, Moses! Yeah, Korach!

WOMAN: Aaron's no good!

NARRATOR: Then the Presence of the Holy One appeared to the whole community.

MOSES: God, it's a mess! Korach is challenging for leadership of the people. He's working up all of Israel against me!

GOD: Stand back. I shall annihilate them.

MOSES AND AARON: Shall the Almighty destroy the good with the wicked?

GOD: Just follow the instructions that I give you.

ANNOUNCER: Now Moses is telling the children of Israel to stand apart from Korach and his company . . . He just promised that something unusual would happen to them . . . He has scarcely finished talking, and the earth is beginning to split! Wow! It's another of those miracles. You have to see this to believe it!

DATHAN: The ground is opening up! Let's get out of here!

NARRATOR: The earth opened its mouth, and all of Korach's people and their possessions and their households were swallowed up. And so God assigned the priesthood to Aaron and his sons, and set off the tribe of Levi for service in the Tabernacle.

* * *

MOSES: Aaron, hurry, offer a sacrifice on behalf of the people! A plague has broken out and thousands of people are dying!

AARON: I will. What shall we do with the fire pans of Korach? Those are holy. They can't be thrown away.

MOSES: Beat the copper pans flat and line the altar with them.

* * *

CHIEFTAIN 1: Moses wants my walking stick.

CHIEFTAIN 2: Mine, too. Can I borrow your knife?

CHIEFTAIN 1: What for?

CHIEFTAIN 2: To carve my name in my walking stick.

CHIEFTAIN 3: This is lunacy. What's he going to do with twelve walking sticks — one from every tribe's chieftain?

CHIEFTAIN 1: Play pick-up sticks?

CHIEFTAIN 2: I think it's another test. He wants to make sure we know who's boss.

CHIEFTAIN 1: I know already. Did you see Korach get swallowed up by the ground? Whoosh! And gone.

CHIEFTAIN 3: He found out that wanting the High Priest job can be a grave undertaking.

NARRATOR: And Moses took the walking sticks of Aaron and of each tribe's chief, and he placed them in the Tabernacle. The next day he brought them out of the Tabernacle and, behold, Aaron's stick had sprouted, producing blossoms and bearing almonds. And Aaron and the Levites took charge of the Holy Sanctuary.

Chukat

חֻקַּת

NUMBERS 19:1-22:1

CAST
PERSON 1
PERSON 2
PERSON 3
PERSON 4
NARRATOR
ANGEL
MIRIAM
ISRAELITE 1
ISRAELITE 2
ISRAELITE 3
MOSES
AARON
GOD
ISRAELITE 4

PERSON 1: The Laws of Uncleanliness.

PERSON 2: A priest who touches or comes into contact with a corpse is unclean for seven days.

PERSON 3: You must cleanse yourself.

PERSON 4: By several different methods stated by Moses. The law of the red cow is difficult to understand. Can you explain how this cow makes the unclean clean, and the clean unclean?

PERSON 1: Nope.

* * *

NARRATOR: Enter Miriam, the prophetess, the brave and clever sister who put Moses in the basket and floated it down the Nile to the Egyptian princess. The sister who followed Moses out of Egypt, and who danced with her maidens when God saved us at the Sea of Reeds.

ANGEL: Miriam, it is your time to go.

MIRIAM: Now? But I haven't seen the Holy Land. I've been in this desert for forty years, give or take a few months. Can't this wait?

ANGEL: Now, Miriam. Your work on earth is complete.

NARRATOR: And so Miriam, sister of Moses and Aaron, died in the land of Kadesh.

* * *

ISRAELITE 1: I am dying of thirst.

ISRAELITE 2: We have been in this desert forever.

ISRAELITE 3: We should have stayed in Egypt.

ALL 3: WE WANT WATER. WE WANT WATER. WE WANT WATER.

MOSES: God, what should Aaron and I do? The people are complaining of thirst.

AARON: It's always something. They are always, always, always complaining!

GOD: You and Aaron take the rod and gather all the Israelites together. Order the rock to bring forth water, and it shall come out.

MOSES: Very well. That sounds easy. Aaron, let's go give them water.

ISRAELITE 1: Look who it is! Moses the miserable who took us out of Egypt.

ISRAELITE 3: Where is the water?

ISRAELITE 2: Boo! Boo! Moses is a liar, a cheat, and a nogoodnik!

MOSES: You ungrateful people! You have seen the power of God, and you still doubt my ability? I am fed up! You want water? Take that!

AARON: Moses, you struck the rock!

MOSES: Of course, I did. I'm angry! Here, watch this. I'll strike it again!

ISRAELITE 4: We are saved! Water is coming forth from the rock as Moses promised!

AARON: Moses, we did it! We got them water! Two whacks on the rock, and splish, splash!

MOSES: We sure did it.

GOD: What do you mean, "we" did it?

AARON: Did I say that? I meant to say, You did it! That's right! God did it!

GOD: You struck the rock instead of speaking to it as I commanded.

MOSES: We were angry! The people were quite rebellious.

GOD: You struck the rock instead of speaking to it, as I commanded.

MOSES: We were doing it for Your glory . . .

GOD: You struck the rock instead of speaking to it, as I commanded.

AARON: Will you forgive us?

GOD: You didn't trust me enough, did you?

AARON: We said we were sorry.

GOD: Because you did not trust in me enough, you will not lead the people into the Promised Land.

MOSES: But God, we have served you for forty years in this desert!

AARON: Forty long, hard, boring years in this desert!

GOD: You have heard the punishment.

NARRATOR: Soon after, Aaron went up to Mount Hor, where he gave the garments of the High Priest to his son Eliezer, and then died.

* * *

ISRAELITE 4: Why did we leave Egypt?

ISRAELITE 2: There is no bread and there is no water. All we have is manna that keeps appearing each morning.

ISRAELITE 3: Why did we leave Egypt just to die in the wilderness?

ISRAELITE 2: We are tired of living in the wilderness!

ALL 4: We want to go back to Egypt!

MOSES: God, they are complaining again.

GOD: A lesson in manners is called for. I will send fiery serpents to bite them.

ALL 4: *(Jumping up and down.)* Ouch, ouch, ouch!

ISRAELITE 1: Moses, tell God we're sorry!

ISRAELITE 3: A lot of people are dying from snake bites. Save us!

GOD: Moses, make a serpent's pole. Any bitten Israelite who looks upon this pole will be healed.

NARRATOR: And so it was that the bronze serpent on a pole healed.

* * *

ISRAELITE 1: Moses, look! We're approaching the land of Moab. We're almost in sight of the Promised Land!

MOSES: I won't be going with you.

ISRAELITE 2: Aren't you bitter?

MOSES: Bitter? No. Forty years in the desert! I have learned to trust in God.

NARRATOR: And the Israelites marched on. And they encamped in the steppes of Moab, across the Jordan River from Jericho. They avoided the way of Ammon and Moab. They met Sihon, the King of the Amorites, and Og, the King of Bashan, and defeated them.

Balak

בלק

NUMBERS 22:2-25:9

CAST
NARRATOR
BALAAM
BALAK
SERVANT 1
GOD
SERVANT 2
DONKEY
ANGEL
ISRAELITE
MOSES

NARRATOR: The story of Balaam and Balak.

BALAAM: I am Balaam, a prophet by profession. *(Bows.)*

BALAK: And I am Balak, king of the Moabites. *(Bows.)*

NARRATOR: And Balak saw the masses of Israelites camping on his borders, and was fearful.

BALAK: This is frightening. As a matter of fact, it's terrifying! Look at all of those Israelites! I must have these people cursed.

NARRATOR: Sifting through the *Moab Sandy Pages*, looking under "Prophets," he came across the name of Balaam.

BALAK: Messengers, go to Balaam and order a curse for the Israelites.

SERVANT 1: Balaam, we come to ask you on behalf of King Balak of Moab to come and curse this people who has camped on our borders.

BALAAM: Will you wait right here? I'll go pack. In the meantime, make yourselves comfortable.

GOD: Balaam, this is the Almighty.

BALAAM: Oh, hello, God. I have a really easy job — all I have to do is curse some Israelites.

GOD: You shall not curse them, for they are blessed.

BALAAM: Please!

GOD: Need I say it twice?

BALAAM: Messengers, tell Balak I will not go to him.

NARRATOR: But Balak was persistent and sent messengers again.

SERVANT 2: Balak says he will reward you richly.

BALAAM: I can't go.

SERVANT 1: Very richly.

BALAAM: I don't think I can go.

SERVANT 2: Very, very richly.

BALAAM: I'll get the donkey ready.

NARRATOR: And so Balaam saddled his donkey and started off. But God was angry, and sent an angel who blocked his way. But the angel who stood with sword in hand was visible only to the donkey.

BALAAM: What is the matter with you? Why have you stopped? I shall beat you for disobeying me!

NARRATOR: Since the donkey still would not move, Balaam tried another path. Once again the angel appeared to block the way. Again the donkey stopped, but only after crushing Balaam's foot against a wall.

BALAAM: You stubborn donkey! I have a good mind to trade you in for a new model. I shall beat you again for disobeying me!

NARRATOR: And the donkey saw the angel again, and she sat down on the road.

BALAAM: I shall beat you again! If I had a sword, I would kill you!

NARRATOR: And God opened the donkey's mouth and she spoke:

DONKEY: Will you put the stick away? Are you crazy? You've put welts all over my back. What in the world did I do to you?

BALAAM: You disobeyed me. You have made a fool of me!

DONKEY: Now look here, I've been giving you lifts everywhere for quite a while. Have I been a good donkey? Yes or no?

BALAAM: Yes.

DONKEY: And if you would have seen an angel of God standing in front of you, what would you have done?

BALAAM: I'd have stopped.

DONKEY: Well, halleluyah! Would you please open your eyes? You have been blind to God. You are in big trouble!

ANGEL: I am an angel of the Almighty One. You could not see what your donkey saw, and so she saved your life.

DONKEY: You tell him, honey!

ANGEL: Go with the men of Moab, but you must listen only to God.

BALAAM: I will do as God commands.

BALAK: Balaam, finally you've arrived! Your curses are known all over the country. Curse the Israelites!

BALAAM: King Balak, I can only speak that which the Almighty One commands. God alone puts words in my mouth.

BALAK: Whatever you say. Come on. Climb up on this hill. Now, look below you — there are the tents of the Israelites. Curse them! Really give it to them! I mean, curse them off the face of this earth. Do your stuff!

BALAAM: I can only bless them.

BALAK: Here, climb over this way. You get a better view from here. Now take a good look and zap 'em!

BALAAM: *Ma tovu ohalecha Ya-akov miskenotecha Yisrael!* How goodly are thy tents, O Jacob, thy dwelling places, O Israel!

BALAK: That's a curse? I'm paying a fortune for cursings and you bless them?

BALAAM: I can only speak as God commands me to speak.

BALAK: You could have been a very rich man.

BALAAM: I could have been a very dead man. I must listen to God.

NARRATOR: And so Balak, king of Moab, dismissed Balaam the prophet from his court. Meanwhile, the Moabites came up with a better plan for destroying the Israelites.

* * *

ISRAELITE: Hey you guys, there are some gorgeous Moabite girls here with nothing to do. Come on!

NARRATOR: And the Israelite men began to worship the god of the Moabite women.

MOSES: God, it appears that we're having some problems.

GOD: Gather all the ringleaders and slay all those who followed the Moabite women.

NARRATOR: And just then, as much of the community of Israel was repenting, an Israelite appeared with a Midianite woman in the sight of Moses.

ISRAELITE: And after a little wine and goat cheese, we can have a candlelight dinner . . .

NARRATOR: And when Pinchas, grandson of Aaron the High Priest, saw this, he grabbed a spear and followed them into their tent and impaled them.

ISRAELITE: Oooooh! He got's me!

NARRATOR: And the Israelites repented. Thus the Almighty's anger was appeased.

Pinchas

פִּנְחָס

NUMBERS 25:10-30:1

CAST
GOD
MOSES
PERSON 1
PERSON 2
PERSON 3
NARRATOR
PERSON 4
ELIEZER
MAHLAH

GOD: Moses, hearken to the voice of God!

MOSES: Yes, Holy One, Blessed be You, I'm here.

GOD: Pinchas has cooled My anger by slaying the Israelite and his Midianite woman.

MOSES: The Midianites have tricked us. Instead of sending an army to fight, they sent their women to tempt us.

GOD: It seems to have worked. Assail the Midianites and defeat them, for they assailed you by trickery.

MOSES: I'll get right on it.

* * *

PERSON 1: And now the Bible . . .

PERSON 2: Brings to you . . .

PERSON 3: The very second census!

NARRATOR: And Moses and Eliezer the priest took a census of the Israelite community, all men from the age of 20 years and up.

PERSON 1: Reuben: 43,730

PERSON 2: Simon: 22,200

PERSON 3: Gad: 40,500

PERSON 4: Judah: 76,500

PERSON 1: Issachar: 64,300

PERSON 2: Zebulun: 60,500

PERSON 3: Manasseh: 52,700

PERSON 4: Ephraim: 32,500

PERSON 1: Benjamin: 45,600

PERSON 2: Dan: 64,400

PERSON 3: Asher: 53,400

PERSON 4: Naphtali: 45,400

PERSON 1: The Grand Total is . . . add the four, carry the one . . . 601,730! That's a lot of people to prepare to enter the Promised Land.

PERSON 2: The Levites, being a holy tribe, which will not receive land in Canaan, aren't included in the census. They numbered 23,000.

NARRATOR: These are the persons enrolled by Moses and Eliezer the Priest on the steppes of Moab. Among these was not one of those enrolled by Moses and Aaron the priest when they recorded Israelites in the wilderness of Sinai. For God had said of them, "They shall die in the wilderness." None survived except Joshua, son of Nun, and Caleb, son of Jephunneh.

MOSES: That about wraps up the census for who gets land in Canaan. Good job, Eliezer!

ELIEZER: Moses, we did it together.

PERSON 4: Excuse me, Mr. Moses. You have visitors.

MOSES: Send the men in.

PERSON 4: They're not men.

MOSES: What do you mean, they're not men. What are they? Cattle?

PERSON 4: They are women.

MOSES: Women? Here? This is unheard of. Oh, very well. Bring them in.

MAHLAH: My name is Mahlah, and these are my sisters — Noah, Hoglah, Milcah, and Tirzah. Our father died in the wilderness and left no sons. Why should his name be lost? Give us a holding among our father's kinsmen.

PERSON 3: The audacity!

PERSON 1: I've never heard of such a thing!

PERSON 2: Next thing you know they'll want the keys to the camel and a tent with a view.

PERSON 4: They must be kidding. Moses, this one is so good, you've got to tell the Almighty.

MOSES: God, these women want to inherit their father's land.

PERSON 1: Isn't that a riot? Can you hear heavenly laughter, Moses? Women owning land!

GOD: That is as it should be. Their plea is just. Give them the hereditary holding. As a matter of fact, make it a law that if a man dies without leaving a son, you shall transfer his property to his daughter.

PERSON 3: Good idea! They get the land.

PERSON 4: I'll go warm up *their* camels.

* * *

GOD: And now, Moses, ascend these heights of Abarim and view the land I have given to the Israelite people. When you've seen it, you too shall be gathered unto your kin, just as Aaron was. For you disobeyed and struck the rock twice to bring forth water.

NARRATOR: And Moses took Joshua, son of Nun, before Eliezer the priest and the whole community, and he invested him with authority so that the Israelites would now follow him.

PERSON 1: Joshua is to take Moses' place as leader of the Israelites when Moses dies.

PERSON 2: These are the laws of the festivals.

PERSON 3: In the seventh month on the first day, you shall observe a sacred occasion. You shall observe it as "a day when the horn is sounded."

PERSON 4: That day is known to us as Rosh HaShanah.

NARRATOR: On the tenth day of the seventh month, you shall observe a sacred occasion when you shall practice self-denial. You shall do no work.

PERSON 1: That day is known to us as Yom Kippur.

PERSON 2: On the fifteenth day of the seventh month, you shall observe a sacred occasion. You shall not work at your occupations. Seven days you shall observe a festival of God.

PERSON 3: That festival is known to us as Sukkot.

PERSON 4: These holidays help us to serve God in truth and righteousness.

PERSON 1: And on the eighth day of the festival of Sukkot . . .

PERSON 2: Weren't there only seven days in Sukkot?

Matot

מַטּוֹת

NUMBERS 30:2-32:42

CAST
ANNOUNCER
MOSES
PERSON 1
CHEERLEADER
NARRATOR
PERSON 2
PERSON 3
PERSON 4
PERSON 5
PERSON 6
ELIEZER
SERVANT

ANNOUNCER: Good morning, ladies and gentlemen! Welcome to an interesting match-up today. Taking the field are the Israelites, and playing defense will be the Midianites. I'll be bringing you the blow-by-blow description as your Bible commentator.

MOSES: All lights are green. The Holy One has instructed me, your captain, to avenge the Israelites against the Midianites. Today, we do it!

PERSON 1: It's about time. We've been talking about this for weeks now.

MOSES: Here's the scoop: I want one thousand men from each tribe to get out there and fight for the honor of Israel!

ALL: Yeah!!!

ANNOUNCER: Well, the mood on the field is electrifying. Moses and Pinchas, son of Eliezer the priest, are deploying their troops with holy vessels and trumpets for alarm.

CHEERLEADER: C'mon! Let's go Israelites! 2, 4, 6, 8, Israelites are really great! 7, 5, 3, 1, Midianites are on the run!

ANNOUNCER: It's a complete victory — at least I think so!

NARRATOR: And the Israelites slew every male.

ANNOUNCER: I would call that somewhat complete. No contest, ladies and gentlemen. It was a complete massacre.

PERSON 1: Hey, Moses, we've captured the women of Midian, their little ones, their cattle and all their flocks and goods.

MOSES: What are you doing with these women?

PERSON 2: We thought we'd bring them along with us.

MOSES: These are the same women that caused us to sin before.

PERSON 1: Oh, but they're sorry. I'm sure they'll apologize. Apologize, ladies.

PERSON 3 AND 4: We're sorry!

MOSES: It doesn't work that way. God has commanded that you slay these women. But harm not the female children.

PERSON 2: But it'll cause such a mess!

PERSON 1: Do you wish the wrath of God upon us? Remember the snakes?

NARRATOR: And the Israelites killed all the males among the little ones, and every woman who had sinned.

PERSON 5: It seems so cruel to kill so many people.

PERSON 6: To us it appears wrong, and by modern standards it would be. However, can we judge accurately the conditions in biblical times?

* * *

ELIEZER: Moses, are you up?

MOSES: Yes. I was just going over the battle reports. The property that we captured from the Midianites has not been distributed. I think we should divide it two ways: half to the warriors, and half to the entire community of Israel.

ELIEZER: And?

MOSES: And everyone will be happy.

ELIEZER: And?

MOSES: Of course, part of it will be taxed for the Holy Tabernacle.

* * *

PERSON 1: I know what he's going to say.

PERSON 2: It doesn't make a difference. It can't hurt to ask.

PERSON 3: You do the talking. We'll support you.

PERSON 1: He's going to say, "Why stop here? You've traveled for forty years."

PERSON 2: We agreed to give it a try.

SERVANT: Welcome to Moses' tent. Do you have an appointment?

PERSON 3: An appointment? Why, no. How silly of us. We'll come back later. We forgot to make an appointment. Oh well!

SERVANT: That's all right. It's a quiet day. You can come right in.

PERSON 1: Is he in a good mood?

SERVANT: In the last four weeks, he has lost Aaron and Miriam and has been denied entry into Canaan for striking a rock instead of speaking to it. I'd say he's a little grumpy.

MOSES: Gentlemen, how can I help you?

PERSON 2: I represent the tribe of Reuben.

PERSON 3: I represent part of the tribe of Manasseh.

PERSON 1: And I represent the tribe of Gad. Moses, seeing this land, where we now have our tents pleases us. Our tribes have much cattle, and we would like to stay on this east bank of the Jordan River instead of crossing over.

MOSES: I don't understand. Why stop here? You've traveled for forty years.

PERSON 1: I told you he'd say that.

PERSON 3: But we like it here.

PERSON 2: We will build cities for our livestock and families, but we will cross over to help conquer Canaan.

MOSES: This sounds reasonable.

NARRATOR: So Moses gave charge of this matter to Joshua and Eliezer the High Priest. And the tribes of Reuben, Gad and the half-tribe of Manasseh said: We will pass over armed before God into the land of Canaan, and the possession of our inheritance shall remain with us beyond the Jordan.

Mas'ay

מַסְעֵי

NUMBERS 33:1-36:13

CAST
SERVANT
MOSES
NARRATOR
PERSON 1
PERSON 2
PERSON 3
PERSON 4

SERVANT: Moses, you should be going to bed soon. It's very late. Hardly an Israelite is up. Even the camels are snoring.

MOSES: I'll be done soon. I'm writing my memoirs. As you know, God will not permit me to enter the land of Canaan. Someone has to record our travels.

SERVANT: Can't it wait?

MOSES: I wish it could. But I could get the call to sleep with my ancestors at any time.

SERVANT: Goodnight, Moses.

MOSES: "The Story of the Israelites in the Desert" by Moses.

NARRATOR: And the Israelites marched out from Egypt while the Egyptians were burying their firstborn. And they camped in Succoth.

PERSON 1: *(The speakers are marching in place.)* From Succoth to Etham.

PERSON 2: From Etham to Pi-hahirot.

PERSON 3: From Pi-hahirot to Pena, and from there to Marah.

PERSON 4: From Marah to the Sea of Reeds.

ALL: The big split.

PERSON 1: From the Sea to Dopka, and then to Alush.

PERSON 2: From Alush to Rephidim, and on to Mt. Sinai.

ALL: The Ten Commandments.

PERSON 3: And from there, we *shlepped* all over the place. And here we are at the steppes of Moab.

PERSON 2: All right, everybody, gather around. I just got back from a meeting with Moses, and he told us that God has instructed that when we cross the Jordan, we must destroy all the people living there and especially all of their idols.

PERSON 3: I'll smash those idols! I'll tear 'em to pieces! I'll crush 'em in my bare hands! I'll mutilate them! Just one question: What's an idol?

PERSON 4: An idol is a piece of wood or stone that people pray to and call god.

PERSON 3: Why would anyone want to pray to a piece of wood?

PERSON 4: Because they don't understand that God is everywhere. Some people still have that problem.

* * *

NARRATOR: And then the Holy One spoke to Moses and gave him the borders of the Promised Land. And God made provisions for those who killed someone accidentally.

PERSON 1: Oh, boy. What do I do? I was out chopping wood with my friend. Enan was standing behind me, and I raised my ax up in the air. I brought it down on the wood, except the blade was gone. I turned around and said, "Enan where's my blade?" But Enan couldn't answer anything. As a matter of fact, poor Enan was dead. The ax head got him. Now his whole family is after me!

PERSON 2: Follow the refuge road!

PERSON 3: Follow the refuge road!

PERSON 4: Follow the refuge road!

PERSON 2: Hello. Have you accidentally killed a friend of yours? Did you mean him no harm? Is his family taking the whole thing rather poorly? Do they want to take an eye for an eye?

PERSON 4: Then you need the city of refuge. That's right, it's just as God commanded. The tribe of Levi manages six cities of refuge. For your convenience we have three on the east side of the Jordan, and three on the west. So if someone is after your hide and you need a place to hide, come to a city of refuge.

PERSON 2: You will be safe from harm as long as you stay within the confines of the city. Don't go out or you're on your own! If the High Priest dies, you are free to return to your land.

PERSON 3: So, you see, the Bible understands that sometimes there are special conditions, even in the case of killing.

PERSON 1: A few more laws about murder. If anyone kills a person, the manslayer must be proven guilty beyond a shadow of a doubt. There must be witnesses.

PERSON 2: And one witness isn't good enough. There must be at least two. They must tell the same story without one contradiction.

NARRATOR: These are the commandments that God gave to the Israelites through Moses on the steppes of Moab, at the Jordan, near Jericho. And a final word on the daughters of Zelophehad: They may marry anyone they wish, so long as he is a member of their tribe. They may not marry anyone who would take their land inheritance away from its tribal borders.

ALL: This concludes the Book of Numbers. *Chazak, chazak, v'nitchazayk* — be strong, be strong, and let us be strengthened.

Devarim

DEUTERONOMY 1:1-3:22

CAST
ANNOUNCER
PERSON 1
MOSES
PERSON 2
PERSON 3
PERSON 4
GOD
NARRATOR
MOABITE
AMMONITES

ANNOUNCER: Ladies and gentlemen, all rise for the leader of the Israelites, that one who split the sea, the one who redeemed the slaves, the one and only . . . Moses! Today, Moses will speak about interesting highlights of his life.

PERSON 1: We've been listening to this guy for days! I wish there was less talking and more action. We can almost see the Promised Land from here.

MOSES: Have I told you about the parting of the sea?

ALL: Yes.

MOSES: What about the Exodus from Egypt?

PERSON 2: We've heard that story, too. Hey, Moses — let's stop the chatter and get on with the conquering of Canaan!

MOSES: I can't go into the Promised Land. Everyone knows that. Have I told you the story of what happened after we left Mount Sinai?

213

PERSON 1: No, I'm sorry to say we have not heard what happened after the Israelites left Mount Sinai.

MOSES: Oh, good. After leaving Mount Sinai, we traveled through the wilderness. Everything was just fine. Everyone was excited about conquering the land of Canaan, when your fathers came to me and said . . .

PERSON 3: Let's send men to spy out the land.

MOSES: I said, no need. God will go before us. But you said . . .

PERSON 4: Listen, we're not walking into some strange land without spying it out first.

MOSES: So we sent spies, and you were all happy. Then they returned and told us that Canaan was inhabited by giants, and we didn't stand a chance of conquering it.

PERSON 1: We saw there a people stronger than we are, and taller, too. They lived in large cities with walls sky high.

MOSES: So God told us: Have no fear or dread of them, because I am the Almighty your God.

PERSON 2: But the spies convinced everyone that it was too dangerous. God grew very angry, and finally said . . .

PERSON 4: I'm going to zap those guys really, really well.

MOSES: God finally decided upon a fair punishment.

PERSON 1: This entire generation of people will die before we enter Canaan.

PERSON 2: Don't you think that's a little harsh?

PERSON 3: Harsh? They had no faith in God. They saw the splitting of the sea, the ten plagues, the giving of the commandments. And after all that wonderful stuff, those stubborn people still doubted God's existence! Not only did they lack faith, they lacked minds. Not one of that evil generation deserved to see the Land promised to our ancestors.

MOSES: After that little episode, the Israelites — your ancestors — felt bad. So they decided that they would try to conquer Canaan, and they gathered an army.

GOD: Moses, tell the people that they shouldn't fight. God's presence will not be with them.

NARRATOR: But nobody listened, and they went up to fight the Amorites.

MOSES: The Amorites defeated the Israelites.

GOD: I told you not to do it.

PERSON 3: Moses, all of this is very interesting, but it's getting late. We would like to begin the conquest of Canaan.

MOSES: I told you before — time is not important. I can't go into Canaan anyway. Back to my story. After 40 years of travel in the desert, everyone was tired and confused.

PERSON 2: Hey, who's got a road map?

PERSON 4: We should be going due east.

PERSON 1: No, no, no! No eastern trail will do. Let's go north.

PERSON 3: Friends, there's no need to bicker. Let's take a look. "A Roadmap from Headquarters Above," or "How to Sneak into Canaan."

NARRATOR: The Israelites passed through the nation of Edom, and the Edomites let them pass. Then the Israelites asked permission to pass through the land of the Moabites, and they replied . . .

MOABITE: Ha, ha, ha. Are you kidding? You want 600,000 people just to come on in? This place would be a mess!

MOSES: We only wish to pass through the land, not conquer it. We will pay for any water we drink.

AMMONITES: We've heard that one before. Suppose that we say no — then are you going to conquer us? Ha!

NARRATOR: So the Israelites went around Moab and Ammon. They went into battle against Sihon, King of the Amorites, and against Og, King of Bashan. And the Israelites were victorious.

MOSES: Well, that about concludes my lecture for today. Next week, we shall continue my series of talks.

PERSON 1: When do we march into Canaan?

MOSES: When Joshua tells you to. For now, pay attention to my lectures on history. They are important. Someday, they'll be put down on paper. They could become a best-seller.

Va'etchanan   וָאֶתְחַנַּן

DEUTERONOMY 3:23-7:11

CAST
MOSES
GOD
NARRATOR
ISRAELITE 1
ISRAELITE 2
ISRAELITE 3
ISRAELITE 4
PERSON 1
PERSON 2
PERSON 3
PERSON 4

MOSES: Ladies and Gentlemen, my name is Moses. I am the leader of the Israelites. I took my people out of Egypt, received the laws of God at Mount Sinai, wandered through the desert for forty years, and fought countless wars along the way. I made one small mistake, though, and for this I am denied permission to enter the Promised Land.

ALL: Our hero!

GOD: Moses, this is God.

MOSES: I've decided to ask You one last time. Please let me cross over the Jordan and see the Land?

GOD: Moses, let's get this straight once and for all.

MOSES: I'll settle for a maybe.

GOD: Enough! Do not speak to Me of this matter again. Go up to the mount of Pizgah and gaze about to the north, south, east, and west. Look at it well, for you shall not cross over the Jordan.

MOSES: Does this mean . . .

GOD: Give Joshua his instructions, for he shall lead this people across into the Land that you may see only from afar.

NARRATOR: And so Moses told the people of Israel all that he had seen and done in the wilderness.

ISRAELITE 1: He talked of the triumphs of God and the Israelites.

MOSES: Remember when you stood before the Almighty your God, when you came forward and stood at the foot of the mountain!

ISRAELITE 2: Look: The mountain is on fire and the flames are touching the sky!

ISRAELITE 3: Listen: God speaks, but there is no shape, only a voice!

ISRAELITE 4: Think: God's words and commandments are holy.

NARRATOR: And it is written in the Bible: Ever since God created man and woman, from one end of the heavens to the other, has anything as grand as this ever happened?

ISRAELITE 1: Has a people ever heard the voice of God through fire and survived?

ISRAELITE 2: Has a God ever taken one nation from the midst of others with wondrous acts as the Holy One our God did for us in Egypt before our very eyes?

ISRAELITE 3: It was done because God loved our fathers and mothers, and chose us from among the nations.

ISRAELITE 4: Observe God's laws and commandments, and keep in mind that the Almighty alone is God in heaven and on earth below.

PERSON 1: Presenting the Ten Commandments — Number One:

PERSON 2: Wow, did I get a good deal on this idol!

PERSON 3: You're not supposed to have idols.

PERSON 2: How come?

PERSON 3: It says, "I am the Almighty your God, who took you out of Egypt. You shall have no other gods beside Me."

PERSON 2: Maybe I can get a refund?

PERSON 1: Commandment Number Two:

PERSON 3: What are you doing?

PERSON 4: I'm painting this beautiful picture of God.

PERSON 3: You can't do that. It says, "You shall not make for yourself any images of God."

PERSON 4: Maybe I can still turn the painting into a landscape of Monterey.

PERSON 1: Commandment Number Three:

PERSON 2: If you don't give me back my camel bag, I swear by the living God . . .

PERSON 3: Do not use God's name in vain.

PERSON 2: Golly, jeepers. Can I pleeease have my camel bag?

PERSON 1: Commandment Number Four:

PERSON 3: Observe the Sabbath and keep it holy.

PERSON 4: Number Five: Honor your mother and father.

ALL: All the time?

PERSON 3: Commandments Six through Ten: You shall not murder. You shall not commit adultery. You shall not steal. You shall not bear false witness. You shalt not be envious of your neighbor's possessions.

PERSON 2: All these precious laws were given to the children of Israel.

NARRATOR: And God said, through Moses, *Shema Yisrael Adonai Elohaynu Adonai Echad.*

MOSES: And the Almighty will bring you into a land flowing with milk and honey. God will dislodge seven nations much larger than you.

ISRAELITE 3: It is not because you are the most numerous of peoples that the Holy One's heart was set on you, and you were chosen. Indeed, you are the smallest of people. But it is because God loved you, and kept the oath made to your ancestors.

MOSES: Therefore, observe faithfully God's laws which I, Moses, charge you this day.

Ekev

עֵקֶב

CAST
NARRATOR
ISRAELITE 1
ISRAELITE 2
MOSES
ISRAELITE 3
ISRAELITE 4
AARON
GOD

NARRATOR: When we last left Moses and the children of Israel, Moses was giving his final words of wisdom to the Israelites as they prepared to enter the land of Canaan.

ISRAELITE 1: Don't forget to turn off the oven. Brush your teeth after every meal. Feed a cold, starve a fever. More whole grains, less red meat. And take your vitamins every day.

ISRAELITE 2: What are you doing?

ISRAELITE 1: I'm practicing. Moses can't live forever. I may be trying out for his job.

ISRAELITE 2: You may be just trying. Oh, here comes Moses now.

MOSES: Okay, Israelites, settle down. I have some announcements to make. First of all, the The Almighty One promises to deliver the land of Canaan unto you. God will help you win this land from the inhabitants, though you are small in numbers.

NARRATOR: And Moses reminded them of all of the trials of the wilderness.

ISRAELITE 3: God gave the Israelites manna in the desert to show that human beings do not live by bread alone, but that people can live on anything that God decrees.

ISRAELITE 4: And the Israelites came unto the foot of Mount Sinai. The mountain was ablaze with fire.

ISRAELITE 3: Moses stayed on the mountain for forty days and forty nights, eating no bread, drinking no water. And the Holy One gave him two tablets of stone, engraved by the finger of God. Do you remember what happened next?

ISRAELITE 1: Aaron, Moses has been gone for forty days. He must be dead.

AARON: No, he is with God.

ISRAELITE 1: But he has no water and no food with him! He's dead.

AARON: Stop saying that. He's just running a little late.

ISRAELITE 2: Let's make our own god.

ISRAELITE 3: We'll make a golden rhinoceros!

ISRAELITE 2: Aaron is a craftsman. He can melt our gold down and carve one.

ISRAELITE 1: He won't do it.

ISRAELITE 2: We'll kill him if he doesn't!

ISRAELITE 1: That might be convincing.

ISRAELITE 3: Then let us build the rhinoceros!

ISRAELITE 2: Gather your gold.

AARON: Wait! What's a rhinoceros?

ISRAELITE 1: You're treading on thin sand.

AARON: One rhinoceros coming up.

ISRAELITE 2: Look, the idol is complete. But it looks more like a calf.

ISRAELITE 3: Good enough. Let's dance and party!

* * *

MOSES: God, I think there is trouble down below. The Israelites have strayed from the path.

GOD: Moses, I shall kill all of them.

MOSES: Please, Holy One, Blessed be You . . . do not destroy them. What would the other nations say about You? What God is it that takes a people out of a land to destroy them in the desert? Remember Your promise to Abraham, Isaac, and Jacob.

NARRATOR: And God listened to Moses, and harmed not the people. And Moses went back up the mountain and received two new tablets. He placed the tablets in the Ark, and the people journeyed onward with the tribe of Levi in charge of the Ark. And Aaron died. Eliezer, his son, became High Priest. And Moses spoke unto the people.

MOSES: And now, O Israel, what does the Almighty your God demand of You?

ISRAELITE 1: Only this — to revere God, to walk only in God's paths, to love God, and to serve God with all your soul and with all your might.

ISRAELITE 2: Protect the fatherless and the widow.

ISRAELITE 3: Be kind to strangers, for you were once strangers in the land of Egypt.

MOSES: The message is clear. God has done wondrous things for the people of Israel. God put up with complaining and rebellion. Follow God's ways, for they will make you better persons, and the world a better place in which to live.

Re'eh

רְאֵה

DEUTERONOMY 11:26-16:17

CAST
MOSES
ISRAELITE 1
ISRAELITE 2
ISRAELITE 3
ISRAELITE 4

MOSES: This day I set before you blessing and curse: the blessing, if you obey the commandments of your God which I enjoin you this day; and the curse, if you do not obey the commandments of your God, but turn away from the path which I enjoin upon you this day and follow other gods. What say you?

ALL: We'll do it! We'll do it!

ISRAELITE 1: Moses, I have a question.

MOSES: Speak up.

ISRAELITE 1: What do we do if we find people worshiping idols?

MOSES: You will destroy all the sites at which others worship their gods. Tear down their altars. Smash their pillars. Cut down the images of their gods.

ALL: We'll do it! We'll do it!

ISRAELITE 1: What if a prophet comes among us and gives us a sign and says, "Let's follow another god?" I mean, I've seen it happen.

ISRAELITE 2: Or, what if your brother or your son or your daughter or your wife or your closest friend says to you secretly, "Come let's worship another god?" I've seen this happen in the desert, Moses.

ISRAELITE 3: Or, what if you settle in a town and there are scoundrels who try to convince you to bow to idols? Oh, Moses, I am afraid! There are so many temptations. What's an Israelite to do? It's a big world out there.

MOSES: Let's talk about love. You can love your new cart. You can love gold and silver. And you can love graven images of gods. All of these things are idols. When you worship gold, it's an idol. What you must truly love is your God.

ISRAELITE 1: Easier said than done. How?

MOSES: By remembering that God took you out of bondage and delivered you from slavery unto freedom. When others tempt you, cast those people from you. Stone them to death, for they are evil.

ALL: We'll do it! We'll do it!

MOSES: What else have you learned?

ISRAELITE 3: These are the animals that the Bible says we can eat. I can say them all in one breath. Ox, sheep, goat, deer, gazelle, roebuck, wild goat, ibex, antelope, mountain sheep, and any other animal that has a cleft foot and chews its cud.

ISRAELITE 2: Take a breath now. That was very good. Where did you learn that?

ISRAELITE 1: At our Holy Tabernacle adult education course. It's open to the public, you know. You ought to sign up.

ISRAELITE 2: Fish.

ISRAELITE 1: I beg your pardon?

ISRAELITE 2: Moses also told us about fish.

ISRAELITE 1: Oh, yes! We can eat anything in the ocean that has fins and scales.

ISRAELITE 2: And we can eat clean birds. Not vultures, eagles, or falcons, though.

ISRAELITE 1: Blech. Who would want to?

ISRAELITE 3: Also, we are not to eat swine. And we shouldn't boil a kid — a baby goat — in its mother's milk.

ISRAELITE 1: Genius! This is pure genius!

ISRAELITE 2: Moses?

MOSES: Come forth.

ISRAELITE 2: Moses, I bring you a poor and needy person.

ISRAELITE 4: I am poor and needy!

MOSES: Poor and needy? The Almighty says: There shall be no needy among you.

ISRAELITE 4: Wow. My mother told me I would be unusual.

MOSES: You shall set aside a tenth of your yield each year unto God. Harden not your heart to the needy. Give willingly. God says: Open your hand to the poor and needy among you.

ISRAELITE 4: I feel cured! I feel happy! I shall no longer be poor and needy! I shall no longer be unusual! Mother will be wrong, for once!

MOSES: Tell me more of what you have learned.

ISRAELITE 2: Observe Passover. For seven days do not eat leavened bread, so you may remember your departure from Egypt.

ALL: Rah!

ISRAELITE 3: From Passover, count off seven weeks and rejoice then in the holiday of Shavuot. A time for remembering the commandments.

ALL: Rah!

ISRAELITE 3: And in the fall, you shall also hold a Festival of Booths, known as Sukkot, to remember the travels in the wilderness.

ALL: Rah!

ISRAELITE 1: And these three times a year, you shall bring gifts unto God for thanksgiving.

MOSES: Well, Israelites, this has been a fine gathering. I'd like to do this more often, but God wants me . . . to straighten out some affairs.

ISRAELITE 1: It was like an adult education class final exam, and we passed!

Shofetim שׁוֹפְטִים

DEUTERONOMY 16:18-21:9

CAST
NARRATOR
ISRAELITE 1
MOSES
ISRAELITE 2
PERSON 1
MANSLAUGHTERER
PERSON 2
PERSON 3
PERSON 4
ANNOUNCER 1
ANNOUNCER 2

NARRATOR: In the previous Sedra (or portion), Moses was addressing the Israelites with his closing thoughts. After forty years in the wilderness, he had a lot to say.

ISRAELITE 1: Moses, you have been talking for five days! Can we take a rest?

MOSES: I have no idea when the Almighty One is coming to take me, so there is not a moment to lose. Now, where was I? Have I talked about justice?

ISRAELITE 2: No. It is a subject yet to be covered.

MOSES: Justice, justice shalt thou pursue, that you may thrive and occupy the land that your God is giving you.

ISRAELITE 1: Which means that before somebody can be put to death, there must be two eyewitnesses. One is not good enough. And if there is the slightest bit of contradiction in the testimonies, there can be no guilty verdict.

ISRAELITE 2: Life is precious, so if there is any doubt of guilt at all, a criminal cannot be put to death.

PERSON 1: Time out, folks. Before we forget, a word for the Levites. Which tribe was not given land in Canaan?

ALL: Which?

PERSON 1: And which tribe must live off the sacrifices given to God?

ALL: Which?

PERSON 1: And which people may live among any other tribe?

ALL: Which?

PERSON 1: The answer, my good friends, is the incredible, awesome tribe of the Levites. Yes, this remarkable family of Levi was chosen by God to serve. Also among their duties, the Levites administer the cities of refuge.

MANSLAUGHTERER: Oh gosh. What do I do? I was out digging a well with my friend, and my ox was standing behind him. I turned around for a moment and accidentally hit the flank of my ox. The ox was startled and moved suddenly, its horn piercing the side of my friend. Woe, woe! My friend fell into the well. All's not well that ends well! He died, and now his whole family is after me. What do I do?

PERSON 2: Follow the refuge road.

PERSON 3: Follow the refuge road.

PERSON 4: Follow the refuge road.

ANNOUNCER 1: Hello, have you accidentally killed a friend of yours? Did you mean him no harm? Is his family taking the whole thing rather poorly? Do they want a life for a life?

ANNOUNCER 2: Then you need a city of refuge. That's right, it's just as God commanded. The tribe of Levi manages six cities of refuge. For your convenience, we have three on the east side of the Jordan River and three on the west. So if someone is after your hide and you need a place to hide, come to a city of refuge!

ANNOUNCER 1: You will be safe as long as you stay within the confines of the city.

ANNOUNCER 2: You will stay in the city until the High Priest dies.

PERSON 1: Matters dealing with war.

PERSON 2: Offer terms of peace to a city before you attack. If they surrender, all the people shall serve you in forced labor. If they choose to fight, put every male to the sword.

PERSON 4: Isn't there a third choice?

PERSON 1: I shall now demonstrate how the Bible asks officers to address their troops.

PERSON 2: All the troops are now gathered. Anyone here who has built a house but has not dedicated his home, leave. Anyone who has planted a vineyard and has not harvested it, leave. Anyone who is soon to be married, leave. And anyone who is afraid, leave.

PERSON 3: Let these people, whose minds are not on battle, leave. The officer then assumes command over the remainder of the troops.

PERSON 2: When you attack a city, do not cut down fruit-bearing trees. Cut down only trees that are not for food.

PERSON 4: We must always strive to be a just people — just to others, and to nature.

Ki Taytzay   כִּי תֵצֵא

DEUTERONOMY 21:10-25:19

CAST
PERSON 1
PERSON 2
PERSON 3
PERSON 4
PERSON 5
PERSON 6
PERSON 7
LAWYER
OX
JUDGE
FATHER
MOTHER
SON
CHAIM
ANAN

PERSON 1: Well, what are the *Sedra* sconcs about this week?

PERSON 2: We already told the story of Moses in the desert, and we acted out the laws and commandments.

PERSON 3: Can't we do more of the same this week, also?

PERSON 4: No, that won't work. *Ki Taytzay* is a difficult *parashah*.

PERSON 5: Why don't we skip it altogether and go straight to the part where Moses dies?

PERSON 4: We can't do that.

PERSON 6: Talking about interest rates and fugitive slaves is not exactly a crowd pleaser.

PERSON 4: True, there are a lot of details in this *Sedra*.

PERSON 7: Worse than that, this chapter goes from end to end with laws. A person can go bananas from so many details!

PERSON 4: But, the laws are important and they can be very interesting. Presenting . . . a world premier . . . of the exciting . . .

PERSON 5: Exciting?

PERSON 4: Electrifying . . .

PERSON 1: Electrifying?

PERSON 4: Incredible *Sedra* of *Ki Taytzuy*!

ALL: Rah, Rah!

LAWYER: I now call the first witness to the stand. State your name.

OX: *(In a Brooklyn accent.)* My name is Max the ox. I woik very hard in de fields every day, and my master, dat brute sitting over dere . . .

LAWYER: Stick to the details.

OX: Very well. Dat callous creature over dere muzzles me. I have to look at all dis food I'm treading on, and I can't eat it! Is dat fair? You lead an ox like me to de corn and you don't have to force me to eat. I'm always ready. Can you believe it? He muzzles me!

JUDGE: That is cruelty to animals. It says that thou shalt not muzzle the animal that treads out the corn. Let the ox eat.

OX: Tanx a lot. I hope you hoid dat, Mister Master.

JUDGE: Next!

FATHER: We bring forth our rebellious son.

MOTHER: He will not listen to our voices.

FATHER: He's a glutton!

MOTHER: He's a drunkard!

FATHER: He's totally uncontrollable!

SON: Yeah, Yeah. I'm a real slob. Don't listen to these hopelessly out of touch parents.

FATHER: Do you see? He talks without respect!

SON: Give me a break . . .

LAWYER: Apparently you do qualify as a rebellious son, according to the Bible.

SON: What do I get? Twenty lashes with a wet noodle? Are my parents gonna spank me?

LAWYER: Actually, according to the Bible, you will be stoned to death.

SON: *(To Judge.)* To death?

JUDGE: To death.

SON: Wow. Like the whole six feet under? Mom, Dad, let's forgive and forget! I'll sit the sheep tomorrow. I'll clean the tent. Can I cook dinner? Italian? Chinese?

JUDGE: I'll take one more case for the day.

CHAIM: Chaim the shepherd, here. I lost these sheep and was looking for them for days. I knew they went past Anan the farmer's house, and so I asked him. He said that he had seen them, but was too busy to gather them together. That's not right.

ANAN: Your honor, the man lives 20 miles away. I'm not going to *shlep* there with his sheep and miss a full day's work.

CHAIM: You pretended you didn't even see them!

ANAN: That's right, and I'd do it again. I've got my own business to tend to.

JUDGE: Gentlemen, the rule is clearly stated. Anan the farmer is wrong. You cannot hide from the lost animals just because it's a hassle. It's your obligation to return the sheep.

ANAN: I don't accept your decision.

JUDGE: Then your punishment is to be beaten.

ANAN: Can't you take a joke? Of course, I admit my mistake. I'm wrong. No doubt about it. Here sheepie, sheepie, sheepie.

PERSON 7: There are a lot more laws in here, but they are "X" rated.

PERSON 4: I told you that the chapter was exciting!

PERSON 7: Some of the important laws not yet mentioned are: if a man gets married, he's excused from military service.

PERSON 1: Don't charge interest to fellow Israelites.

PERSON 2: Be kind to the stranger, the orphan, and the widow.

PERSON 3: Don't marry your stepmother.

PERSON 4: Be kind to people who own no land.

PERSON 7: *Ki Taytzay* talks about the responsibilities we have to ourselves and to our fellow man and woman.

PERSON 1: There sure are a lot of laws in this chapter!

Ki Tavo

כי תבוא

DEUTERONOMY 26:1-29:8

CAST
JOSHUA
LEVITE
JUDAH
SIMON
BENJAMIN
DAN
NARRATOR

JOSHUA: Are you sure this is what we are supposed to do today?

LEVITE: Positive.

JOSHUA: We have half the Israelites standing on Mount Gerizim, and the other half are facing them on Mount Ebal.

JUDAH: Hey, move over. This mountain is getting crowded!

SIMON: You move over. We have to get 300,000 people on this mountaintop.

LEVITE: I bet we're going for the Guinness Book of Biblical Records. I heard that the Egyptians once got half a million people into a riverboat.

BENJAMIN: Someone is standing on my toe! Hey, that's *my* head you're scratching!

JOSHUA: Are you sure Moses commanded us to put six tribes on each mountaintop?

LEVITE: It's right here in the Book. It says, and I quote: Moses charged the people, saying: After you have crossed the Jordan, the following will stand on Mount Gerizim, and the following shall stand on Mount Ebal . . .

DAN: That was some climb. Look at all these people!

JUDAH: Are you sure you are in the right place?

DAN: I think so. I'm from the tribe of Dan.

JUDAH: Out of luck. Your tribe is on the other mountain.

DAN: Their mountain looks more squished than this one. Hey, Joshua, wait a minute. I have to change mountains.

JOSHUA: Hurry up! Okay, what do we do now?

LEVITE: According to Moses' instructions, we are to recite curses and blessings.

JOSHUA: Let's have some quiet. We have some curses and blessings to give out, and we need everyone's attention. That way, nobody can say, "I didn't hear that."

SIMON: All these people together makes me feel like I'm at a football game. And having to answer "Amen" after each curse makes me think of the cheerleaders.

JUDAH: I would hardly compare the Levite priests who recite the curses to cheerleaders!

NARRATOR: And the Levites proclaim in a loud voice to all who stood on Mt. Ebal . . .

LEVITE: Cursed be he who insults his mother or father.

ALL: Amen!

LEVITE: Cursed be he who takes advantage of strangers, widows, and orphans.

ALL: Amen!

SIMON: Go Pittsburgh!

JUDAH: Pittsburgh?

SIMON: Ooops. I got carried away. I told you this reminds me of a football game — this is like the pep rally!

JOSHUA: If you are good and follow God's teachings, your country will be blessed. So will your animals and crops. God will give you victory over your enemies. It will rain when it is supposed to, and all will go well with you.

BENJAMIN: I have a question. What happens if we don't listen to the teachings of God?

JOSHUA: Let me check that out. Here it is. The Bible says: If you disobey, God will punish your cities, let loose fever, drought, mildew, heat waves, pestilence, and boils.

BENJAMIN: Oh, is that all? I'm so glad I asked.

JOSHUA: No, there's more. God will turn the earth to dust, strike you with madness, blindness, and dismay, and you'll be robbed and plundered.

SIMON: You can stop now. You're depressing us.

JOSHUA: But there's more . . .

JUDAH: We get the idea. We'll be good.

JOSHUA: God will send a mighty nation to destroy you. You will be scattered across the earth and find no peace.

BENJAMIN: Stop! I can't take so much good news at one time.

LEVITE: Do we get to choose between the blessing and the curse?

JOSHUA: I think it's up to us.

JUDAH: It's such a tough choice. Do I want to be plagued with fever, drought, and madness, or do I want my land to prosper? Decisions, decisions!

JOSHUA: Just remember, this applies to future generations as well. On this day we witnessed what the consequences will be. On this day we bear testimony to God's will.

SIMON: With 300,000 people stuck together, testimony is the easiest thing to bear.

JOSHUA: Why do I get the feeling that God is going to look back on this day and say, "I told you this would happen"?

LEVITE: Can we get off the mountain now?

DEUTERONOMY 29:9-30:20

CAST
SERVANT
MOSES
GUARD
LADY
MAKEUP
ANNOUNCER

SERVANT: Knock, knock. Mr. Moses?

MOSES: Come in.

SERVANT: The people are all ready.

MOSES: Is everyone here?

SERVANT: It's standing room only. I saw tribal leaders, elders, officials, Israelites and their families, and even some strangers.

MOSES: That is some crowd!

SERVANT: What will you talk about tonight?

MOSES: I have several things to tell the people, and time is short.

SERVANT: People love it when you remind us of our covenant with God, and when you talk about how people who worship false gods will be punished.

MOSES: Okay. I'll begin with that.

SERVANT: I'm great at suggestions like that. Can I be one of your writers?

MOSES: Sorry, son. Only one writer handles my lines, and God is all that I need.

GUARD: Miss, you can't go in there!

LADY: I have to!

GUARD: This is Moses' private tent.

LADY: Let me pass or I'll scream!

SERVANT: What's going on out here?

GUARD: This lady wants to see Moses.

LADY: I have to see you, I just have to! It's vital! It's critical! It's important.

MOSES: Yes, come in. What is it?

LADY: Moses, can I have your autograph?

GUARD: That's what's so important?

LADY: It's not for me, it's for a sick friend. Please sign. Come on. Put a *mem, shin, hey* down on the tablet.

MOSES: *(Signs her tablet.)* There you go.

LADY: Thanks! One other thing. Will you talk about how God's heart will open to the Israelites, and God will bring them back from the corners of the earth? And how God will make us numerous and prosperous? It's my very favorite speech of yours!

MOSES: Yes, I shall.

LADY: Oh, I'm going to love it — it's so exciting! Oooh!

MAKEUP: Mr. Moses, time for makeup.

SERVANT: Must he put that stuff on?

MAKEUP: Yes. Ever since he encountered God, his face shines so radiantly that we all need sunglasses to look at him.

SERVANT: Very well, but hurry.

MAKEUP: I'd like to make a request. Would you talk about loving God, walking in God's ways, and keeping God's laws? I love that sermon. And then you say, you've all got a choice — the blessing or the curse. Therefore, choose life and love God. Oh, that's my very favorite line.

MOSES: Yes, I was going to say that to the people.

SERVANT: The people are waiting.

ANNOUNCER: Ladies and gentlemen, here he is, that lovable leader, your favorite and mine, Mr. Bring Down the Tablets himself, Moses!

LADY: Oooh! He's going to talk about the good times.

MAKEUP: Love and choices — listen.

SERVANT: I read his speech. He's going to talk about our covenant with God and how it applies to everyone. But he better do it quick. It's a short *Sedra*.

MOSES: . . . so listen to the Almighty your God, that you and your children after you will dwell in the land which God swore to Abraham, Isaac, and Jacob to give us.

SERVANT: The audience loves it!

MAKEUP: The makeup does it every time.

LADY: Did I ever tell you how I got Moses' autograph?

Vayaylech

וַיֵּלֶךְ

DEUTERONOMY 31:1-30

CAST
NARRATOR
MOSES
JOSHUA
ISRAELITE 1
ISRAELITE 2
GOD
LEVITE

NARRATOR: Good afternoon, ladies and gentlemen! We are broadcasting to you live from the Israelite camp where Moses, the great leader of his people, is preparing his farewell address.

MOSES: I am 120 years, old and can no longer come in and go out as before.

JOSHUA: You have the strength of a dozen men, Moses! We wish you would live forever.

MOSES: I'm pleased that God selected you as the next leader of the Israelites, Joshua.

JOSHUA: I'm also glad God selected me.

NARRATOR: Moses has come out of the tent with his faithful friend Joshua by his side. The Israelites are silent. They know that Moses will soon die. The first words out of Moses' mouth are eagerly anticipated. What wisdom will Moses share with them today?

MOSES: I am now one hundred and twenty years old, and can no longer be as active . . .

ISRAELITE 1: THAT'S what he called us here to tell us? It doesn't take much to figure out that at 120 Moses is slowing down!

ISRAELITE 2: I've never heard anyone open a speech like he did. What ever happened to words like "I've come to bury Caesar, not praise him," "Four score and seven years ago," "When in the course of human events," or "A chicken in every pot"?

MOSES: I will not be going across the Jordan River to help conquer Canaan. Instead, Joshua will lead you, and our nation shall triumph over anyone who stands in our way.

NARRATOR: Then Moses called Joshua into the sight of all Israel.

MOSES: This is Joshua. He shall take my place as your leader. Be strong and of good courage, and the Almighty God will go before you. Now, say something to the people.

JOSHUA: Uh . . . uh . . . what is expected of me?

MOSES: Don't worry, Joshua. I'm writing everything down, and I'll give it to the priests to hold onto.

GOD: Moses . . .

MOSES: Just a minute, Holy One, Blessed be You. I want to make sure I've told the people everything I have to. I'm checking . . . Be good, walk with God . . . check. Seeing someone's ox in the road, don't ignore it . . . check. Every seventh year . . . almost missed that. Listen, my people; in the seventh year at the Feast of Booths, you are to gather and read the Torah in the presence of everyone . . .

GOD: Moses, it's time to go.

MOSES: At 120 years old? I'm still in my prime!

247

GOD: Moses, it is almost time for you to die. Bring Joshua and present yourselves to Me at the Tent of Meeting.

NARRATOR: And the Almighty appeared at the Tent in the pillar of cloud.

JOSHUA: I'm a bit nervous. In fact, I'm scared.

LEVITE: Settle down, kid. You want to be in the big leagues, you better get used to the Manager.

GOD: Moses, after the people enter the Land, they will forget Me and will break the covenant. They shall suffer. Therefore, write down this poem and teach it to the people of Israel, so that when they go astray they shall remember why they are suffering.

MOSES: I have the poem all written down as You asked.

NARRATOR: And Moses went to the Levites who carried the Ark of the Covenant and said . . .

MOSES: I'd like to have you hold this Book of teachings in the Holy Ark. It will be safe there.

LEVITE: Thank you.

MOSES: This Book shall be a witness to what will be.

NARRATOR: Moses ordered the elders and officials to be gathered to him to hear the words of the poem.

ISRAELITE 1: I just love poetry readings! This should be fun.

ISRAELITE 2: Poetry can be so thrilling, don't you agree? Shhh. Moses is going to start.

MOSES: When I am no more, you will act wickedly and turn from the right path. In time, misfortune will befall you.

ISRAELITE 1: Maybe we shouldn't have come to this poetry recital.

Ha'azinu

CAST
ANNOUNCER
ISRAELITE 1
MOSES
ISRAELITE 2
ISRAELITE 3
NARRATOR
GOD

ANNOUNCER: Ahem, ahem. Ladies and gentlemen! May I have your undivided attention? We have a very special treat today. As you know, Moses will not be with us much longer.

ISRAELITE 1: He can be so blunt! Must you rub it in?

ANNOUNCER: You're the one who asked me to introduce Moses' farewell address. It is a *farewell* address, isn't it?

MOSES: Actually, it's a poem. I wrote it myself.

ANNOUNCER: How fabulous! Shh. Everyone, please settle down. Today Moses will do a poetry recital. These will be his last few words before he dies.

ISRAELITE 1: Oy! Try to be subtle.

ANNOUNCER: All right, all right. Let me introduce the poem. What is it called?

MOSES: I call it . . . *Ha'azinu.*

ANNOUNCER: Now, here's "Moses' Last Will and Testament."

ISRAELITE 2: What's going on up there?

ISRAELITE 3: It's hard to tell. You would think they'd install a better sound system when 600,000 people show up for a poetry recital. Everybody could hear loud and clear at Mount Sinai.

ISRAELITE 2: True, but you know who installed the sound system for *that* event. Shhh. I think Moses is beginning the poem.

NARRATOR: Then Moses recited the words of the poem to the very end, in the hearing of the whole congregation of Israel.

MOSES: Give ear, O heavens, let me speak. Let the earth hear the words I utter.

ISRAELITE 2: Nice opening, I like it. Moses is off to a good start.

MOSES: God found Jacob in a desert region . . . God surrounded Israel and watched over him, guarded him . . . like an eagle who protects its nestlings.

ISRAELITE 3: That is so well put. God's an eagle and we are the protected ones. I feel safe and secure. Moses is really rolling now!

MOSES: But you will forget and forsake God and will be punished.

ISRAELITE 2: I knew there was a catch. Punishment! Wow, we have something to look forward to in the future.

MOSES: In the end, God will save you from your enemies after you realize that there is truly only one God.

ISRAELITE 3: I love a happy ending, don't you?

GOD: Moses, this is God.

MOSES: God, were You at the poetry recital?

GOD: Moses, I am everywhere. How could I miss it? You were wonderful. Now, ascend Mount Nebo and view the land of Canaan, which I am giving to the Israelites.

MOSES: I'd rather wait and see it when I've crossed into the Land.

GOD: You broke faith with Me and struck the rock. You cannot enter the Land.

MOSES: I was hoping that You forgot about that.

GOD: You shall not enter the Land, Moses, but you shall see it all from Mount Nebo.

V'zot
HaBrachah

DEUTERONOMY 33:1-34:12

CAST
NARRATOR
MOSES
ISRAELITE 1
ISRAELITE 2
DAN
ASHER
GOD

NARRATOR: Ladies and Gentlemen, this is the last section of the last book of the Torah. Moses has talked all the way through the book of Deuteronomy.

MOSES: In conclusion . . .

ISRAELITE 1: Did he say, "In conclusion"? Am I dreaming, or did he say "In conclusion"?

ISRAELITE 2: Forty years can just fly by when you're having fun.

MOSES: The Almighty came from Sinai and shone from Seir upon them. At God's right hand was a fiery law unto them.

ISRAELITE 1: My parents told me about that. Boy, that must have been cool! When my Dad described it, I could almost see that smoke and fire and Moses smashing the tablets. That must have been some experience!

MOSES: I shall now bless the tribes of Israel. Are you ready? Are the leaders of the tribes here? Reuben. Let Reuben live and not die, since they are few in number.

ISRAELITE 2: I told you that Zero Population Growth was going to catch up with us.

MOSES: Judah, you're all right. You shall be a leader. Levi, teach the people the law and practice it. You have proven yourselves. You will do well. Benjamin, you're beloved of God. Now comes Joseph.

ISRAELITE 1: I'll bet this is going to be one sweet blessing.

MOSES: Let blessing be upon the head of Joseph and upon the crown of the head of him that is a prince among his brothers.

ISRAELITE 2: Once a favorite, always a favorite.

MOSES: Zebulun, you're okay. Issachar will call the peoples to the mountain. Gad will grow in number. Dan will be like a lion's whelp.

DAN: A lion's whelp? What is that supposed to mean?

ISRAELITE 1: Young and spry. All body, but a tad off in smarts and experience. You'll learn, though.

MOSES: Naphtali shall posses the sea, and Asher shall be blessed above his brothers and shall dip his foot in oil.

ASHER: Wow! We get to dip our feet in oil!

ISRAELITE 1: Relax, it's just an expression. Like . . . you're rolling in dough. It's good.

MOSES: Happy are you, O Israel! Who is like you? A people saved by God.

NARRATOR: And Moses went up from the plains of Moab to Mount Nebo, and God showed him all the Land.

GOD: This is the Land which I swore to your fathers Abraham, Isaac, and Jacob. I have caused you to see it, but you shall not enter the Land.

MOSES: It's been quite a life.

GOD: You have done all that was asked of you.

NARRATOR: And Moses, the servant of God, died there in the land of Moab. He was 120 years old. The children of Israel wept for Moses for thirty days. Never has a prophet arisen in Israel like Moses, whom God knew face to face, in all the signs and the wonders that the Holy One sent him to do in the land of Egypt, to Pharaoh, and to his servants, and to all God's people Israel.

ALL: This concludes the Book of Deuteronomy. *Chazak, chazak, v'nitchazayk* — be strong, be strong, and let us be strengthened. Next week we begin the Torah again — are you ready?